Search Engine Society

Digital Media and Society Series

Mark Deuze, *Media Work*
Alexander Halavais, *Search Engine Society*
Robert Hassan, *The Information Society*
Tim Jordan, *Hacking*
Jill Walker Rettberg, *Blogging*

Search Engine Society

ALEXANDER HALAVAIS

polity

First published in 2009 by Polity Press

Polity Press
65 Bridge Street
Cambridge CB2 1UR, UK.

Polity Press
350 Main Street
Malden, MA 02148, USA

ISBN-13: 978-0-7456-4214-7
ISBN-13: 978-0-7456-4215-4 (paperback)

A catalogue record for this book is available from the British Library.

Typeset in 10.25 on 13 pt FF Scala
by Servis Filmsetting Ltd, Stockport, Cheshire
Printed and bound in Great Britain by MPG Books Ltd, Bodmin, Cornwall.

For further information on Polity, visit our website: www.polity.co.uk.

Contents

Introduction

Take a moment and type the following search query into your favorite search engine: "Google is your friend." Today, the number of hits on Google stands at "about 474,000." The company is successful, but who knew it was so friendly? Even the abbreviation of the phrase – GIYF – receives about 19,300 hits. If you have picked up this book, you can probably guess the context in which this phrase is used. If not, a description may be found at http://fuckinggoogleit.com/, which reads, in part:

Google Is Your Friend

All Smart People Use Google

It Appears That You Are Not One Of Them

The search engine has become so much a part of our culture that there is a common assumption that we have found a cure for stupid questions. Folded into that assumption we find a host of others: that even the unintelligent have access to and can use a search engine, that a search engine will lead someone to a page that contains accurate information, and that questions are best directed first to a machine, and only after that to other people.

This book suggests that those assumptions are dangerously flawed; that unpacking the black box of the search engine is something of interest not only to technologists and marketers, but to anyone who wants to understand how we make sense of a newly networked world. Search engines have come to play a central role in corraling and controlling the ever-growing sea of information that is available to us, and yet they are trusted more readily than they ought to be. They freely provide, it seems, a sorting of the wheat from the chaff, and answer our most profound and most trivial questions. They have become an object of faith.

We ask many things of search engines, what do they ask in return? Search engines are at once the most and the least visible part of the digital, networked revolution. The modern search engine has taken on the mantle of what the ancients of many cultures thought of as an oracle: a source of knowledge about our world and who we are. Children growing up in the twenty-first century have only ever known a world in which search engines could be queried, and almost always provide some kind of an answer, even if it may not be the best one.

Search engines appear to be merely a functional tool, aimed at making the real work of the web easier, but they have the potential to reveal to us not only their internal structures, but the internal structures of the societies that build them. In *Troilus and Cressida*, Shakespeare (1912, p. 35) hints at why an examination of search engines is so enticing:

> And in such indexes, although small pricks
> To their subsequent volumes, there is seen
> The baby figure of the giant mass
> Of things to come at large.

Search engines represent the screens through which we view the content of the web, screens that allow us to inflict our own desires on the "giant mass" of the web, taming it and making it useful. At the same time, the view it presents is likely to shape future social values.

In his book *Information please*, Mark Poster (2006) reminds us of the change that has occurred: we once asked people for information and now we ask machines. He is interested in how this change to machine-mediated information affects our interactions. But it is all too easy to forget that the machines we are asking are constructed in ways that reflect human conceptions and values.

As with any kind of filter, this book comes with a bias. That bias should be clear throughout, but to make it more findable, I state it plainly here. People who use search engines – and that is slowly approaching "everyone" – should know how they work, and what they mean to society. Once they know this, they will recognize the need to take collective action and participate in the management of these technologies. The appropriate search engine does not promote authoritarian dominion over knowledge, but invites communal finding and search sociability.

The first and second chapters introduce the basic mechanics of search engines and how users employ them. At a very basic level, understanding how to effectively search using a search engine requires that we know how the system collects information and how it is best accessed. But understanding this raises further questions. In the third chapter, we visit the trenches of search engine optimization and agonistic attempts to rise in search engine rankings. While the average searcher may not recognize what goes into the collection and ranking of pages on the web, industries that thrive on attention are far more aware of the process and how it might be manipulated. In chapter 4, it becomes clear that the structure of the web, and its representation through search engines, challenges visions of a platform that encourages democratic discussion.

During the early years of the search engine, governments were nearly as blind to their role as most users. Particularly in the last few years, search engines have become embroiled in substantial policy dilemmas. In particular, interactions with national governments have resulted in search engine censorship of various forms (as discussed in chapter 5), and intrusions on personal privacy (in chapter 6). Each of these hints at deeper questions of interactions between the traditional authority of governments and the new power of search engines. In the latter case, they may also mark a shift in how we identify as individuals within our own communities.

Given these challenges, what hope is there for more accountability in search? Chapter 7 addresses the new forms of "sociable search," search systems that incorporate not only collective searching, but searching that leads to community. The oft-remarked shift on the web from static publishing to user-created media and collaborative sites, including collaborative filters and collaborative tagging, provides new, more inclusive avenues for searching and finding. The final chapter ventures to suggest some areas in which search technology is expanding, and some of the ways in which those changes may relate to social changes in the next decade and beyond.

This is an important moment in the history of search engines, the internet, and a networked global society. Search engines emerged as the epicenter of the early web, and represent a nexus of control for the future. Those who recognize their power, and are able to exercise control over it, will help to shape our collective future.

CHAPTER ONE

The Engines

It is tempting to treat the search engine as a free-standing technology, an invention that has made it easier to find things located on another independent technology, the World Wide Web. But even a cursory investigation suggests that the search engine, like most other technologies, is not something that can be treated without reference to a larger social context, and to evolutionary social and cultural changes. The search engine, far from being an isolated modern artifact, represents a touchstone of digital culture, and a reflection of the culture in which it exists.

This chapter provides a brief overview of what a search engine is and where it comes from, and a sketch of the industry that supports it, before outlining a few of the social changes it might represent. By understanding the historical, social, technological, and cognitive contexts of the search engine, we are better able to triangulate toward an understanding of the technology, toward an indication of the place of the search engine in our world and what it portends. The permanent loss of search engines is now almost unfathomable, but were it to occur, we would find the way we communicate, learn about the world, and conduct our everyday lives would be changed. And so we must look beyond the familiar "search box" and understand what it reveals and what it conceals.

Search engines today

A basic definition of the search engine might refer to an information retrieval system that allows for keyword searches of distributed digital text. While a search engine is usually a system that indexes webpages, the term has been extended more broadly to include a range of information environments and media forms, including multimedia and other content found on restricted intranets and individual computers. If you ask someone what a search engine is, however, they are less likely to provide a definition than they are to indicate one of the handful of top search engines that represent some of the most popular sites on the web: Google, Yahoo, Microsoft Live, or Ask.com, for instance.

And these sites are popular. Google is easily the most popular search engine today, and the various Google sites, including its search engine, are among the most popular sites on the web. According to one measure, Google properties are the most visited sites of any kind in the world, ranking first in the United Kingdom, France, and Germany (comScore July 1, 2007). They rank third in the United States, closely trailing sites owned by Yahoo and Time-Warner, and rank third behind Yahoo and Microsoft in Asia (comScore July 9, 2007). A listing of the most popular search engines globally appears in table 1.1. A Pew Internet and American Life study carried out in 2005 found that search engine visits were growing rapidly among American users, approaching the frequency of the most popular use of the internet, email (Rainie 2005). There can be little doubt that visits to search engines make up a large

Table 1.1 Global search engine use as of July 2007	
Search engine	Global share
Google	53.3%
Yahoo	20.1%
MSN/Live	13.6%
AOL	5.2%
Ask	1.8%
Others	6.0%

Source: Nielsen//NetRatings, as cited in Sullivan (2007)

part of internet use, though it can be difficult to discover just how frequent that use is, and for what reasons.

One reason for this difficulty is that people often encounter the large search engines through the façade of another site; that is, without intending to. So a search on a particular website may rely on Google to do the actual searching, or it may draw on an internal search engine. Both of these are a form of search, but may be measured differently by different research firms (Hargittai 2004). Many portal sites are also search engines, so just measuring the visitors, for example, to Yahoo properties does not provide a useful metric of actual searches. As hard as measuring the use of public search engines is, it is nearly impossible to measure search more generally: people searching their company intranet or their hard drive, for example.

Particularly in recent years, there has been a rise in specialized search engines that seek to index not the entire web, but some constrained portion. This is often referred to as "vertical search," as opposed to the "horizontal search" of the general purpose search engines. Topically constrained search engines seek out only pages within a particular knowledge domain, or of a particular type of content. Some of these sites are efforts to move databases that have traditionally been found in libraries onto the web. ScienceDirect, for example, provides reference to scientific literature for web users, and Google Scholar provides the utility of a large article and citation index provided by scholarly journals combined with scholarly sources from the web. Some of these vertical search engines are focused on a particular industry. For example, an attorney in the United States might turn to open sources like FindLaw to provide news and information about their practice, to Lawyers.com to find an attorney within a particular practice area, or to THOMAS, a search engine maintained by the federal government to track legislation, in addition to a number of subscription-based search engines for legal information like Westlaw and Lexis-Nexis.

Some niche search engines focus on a specific geographical area. "Local search" has taken over the function of many local telephone directories, providing information about local serv-ices. Rather than competing with local search, many of the largest business directories ("yellow pages") have created their own local search engines, as have local newspapers and televi-sion stations. Local search is often combined with mapping services, and there is an opportunity to create what is often called "locative media," providing information that depends on the geographical context of the individual, determined through GPS and other mobile devices. Others cater to particular modes of delivery; Google, for example, offers information about local business via voice for telephone users (Cheng 2007).

Sometimes it is not the content area that determines the search, but the type of media. Although large search engines, beginning with AltaVista, generally have had some ability to search for multimedia, it continues to present some of the greatest challenges, and some of the greatest opportunities for those creating vertical search engines. Sweden's Polar Rose, for example, seeks to use face-recognition technology to iden-tify individual people in photographs on the web (Schenker 2006). Right now, searchers have to rely on accurate sur-rounding text, which may or may not identify individuals in the photographs, but this opens up photographs on the web in a whole new way.

Some of these efforts toward vertical search are created by groups with a particular interest in a certain narrow topical or geographical area; a good search engine may be seen as a way of promoting a particular topic, language, or region. Alternatively, for those who wish to create new kinds of search engines, it may make sense to try to capture a smaller audi-ence, rather than go into head-to-head competition with the giants, at least in the early stages (Regan 2005). In many cases, however, the giants are now creating their own niche sites, or acquiring sites that show potential, in order to dominate the entire search market and integrate their services.

Many of the new approaches to cataloging the web attempt to leverage search technologies by combining them with tacit and explicit coding of content by individual web surfers. While the taxonomic structures of some web directories, or the tagging structures of "folksonomic" sites like Flickr and del.icio.us, may seem to represent alternatives to search engines, in fact they both depend on the idea of search, and enhance search functionality. Many search engines trace the search behavior and even the surfing behavior of their users to better anticipate effective search results, or to better organize their indexes. Though the initial search engines marked a move away from human coding, clever engines now extract patterns from their users to exploit their social sense of what is an appropriate search result. It is likely that search will continue to become more closely tied to social relationships, moving to provide information not only about text, but about people who may have the expertise a searcher is seeking.

Although they may not be called "search engines," these technologies extend into even narrower domains. Early websites gradually adopted the practice of tree-like organizational structures, and eventually other ways of indexing content on the site. Especially after about 2000, though, the search box became a fixture on most sites of any size. Not only do people expect to see a search box, they expect it to behave in standard ways; anything outside of the expected will frustrate the average web user (Nielsen 2005). The search engine is now ingrained in our web experience, appearing as a box in the corner of e-commerce sites, personal blogs, dating sites, hospital websites, and nearly everything in-between.

Search engines have recently reached beyond the web. Of course, there have always been large collections of data that needed to be indexed in some way, particularly in libraries, but the specific technologies developed for search engines are now frequently to be found as a way of seizing hold of otherwise unmanageable unstructured and heterogeneous stores of data: email, documents, and the entire contents of home computers and corporate networks. As our use of digital media converges, mixing and combining computing applications with more traditional media, we also find search engines becoming a part of our entire media ecosystem. It might once have been considered odd to search for a specific piece of information among a friend's collected email correspondence, a week's worth of your own television viewing, a novel, or the address book on your mobile telephone, but search is now becoming an expected feature of many previously unindexed collections of data.

Because the web is becoming an ever-expanding database of human knowledge, it represents the greatest challenge for those wishing to create systems to collect, summarize, organize, and retrieve information. Naturally, these tasks have existed before, but the size, extent, and diversity of the content of the web make it the ultimate target for such efforts. As a result, those who would have studied other topics in artificial intelligence, information design, library science, and a host of other fields have set their sights instead on developing a better search engine.

Before the search engine

Some consider the greatest modern threat to be too much information, a glut of data that obscures what is really valuable. In his book *Data smog*, David Shenk (1997, p. 43) argues that computers are the "most powerful engines driving the information glut" by constantly drawing more data to our attention. While it is undoubtedly the case that the internet allows for the rapid delivery of ever growing amounts of information, it is also true that new computing devices were often created in order to manage and control increasingly complex environments. What once could be handled by a human, or a collection of individuals, became too time-consuming to result in effective control. So in 1823, when the British government recognized the need for an effective replacement for human "calculators" to come up with tide tables at their ports, they funded an effort by Charles Babbage to design the first mechanical computer (Campbell-Kelley & Aspray 1996). Likewise, when the United States government found that it would take more than ten years to tabulate the decennial national census in 1890, they turned to Herman Hollerith, who founded the company that later became IBM, to create an automatic tabulating system (Aul 1972). That pattern of turning to information technology when faced with an overwhelming amount of data has occurred over and over: in libraries, in large businesses, and, eventually, on the World Wide Web.

It is natural to think of information technology as digital computing, since so much of contemporary information processing is relegated to networked computers. Computers are only the most recent in a long line of technologies that were created to allow for better control of complex collections and flows of information. The obvious example is the library: once a collection of books and papers grows to a significant size, finding the appropriate piece of information in a timely manner becomes the subject of its own techniques, records, and machinery. Collections of documents can be traced back nearly as far as history itself has been recorded; were cave drawings the first private libraries? As Kaser (1962) explains, many spiritual traditions conceive of the library as eternal, and the librarian as all-powerful. As early private collections grew larger, librarians emerged to organize and manage these collections. Because libraries were so important to many classical civilizations, the librarian was in a revered and politically powerful position which required special skills in collecting and manipulating information. Large libraries have always been a nexus of potential information overload, and so techniques and technologies evolved to help us filter and find information.

Sorting and finding items within these collections required the creation and maintenance of information about the collection: metadata. The Babylonian library at Nippur had such records of the collection as early as the twentieth century BCE. The nature of the need was simple enough: the librarian needed to be able to discover which books or documents addressed a given topic, and then find where that book was physically located so that it could be retrieved for the person requesting information. Given that the subject of a work was often the issue most closely indexed to an informational need, the most popular indexes in the English-speaking world – the Dewey Decimal system and the Library of Congress System – provide a classification that is based on the subject matter of a book, so that books on similar topics are likely to be found in close proximity.

The use of computing systems in libraries has formed an important basis for how search engines now work. There is a long history of ideas about how to organize knowledge in the library, but the rise of computing in a library setting brought mathematics and linguistics to bear in new ways, and many of the techniques now used by search engines were first used by library indexes. The field of Information Retrieval (IR) now bridges the closed library index and the wider collection of documents on the web (Salton 1975), and draws from many areas of computing and information science to better understand the information available over computer networks.

Public and private libraries were not the only form of data collections. The industrial revolution led to new forms of social organization, particularly the rise of bureaucracy, which required a flood of new paper files. Records and copies of correspondence were generally kept on paper, and guides emerged for suggesting the best ways to organize these materials, including the best ways to stack papers on a desk. Paper stacking gave way to pigeonholes, and the business titans of the early twentieth century made use of a fabulously expensive piece of office furniture called the "Wooton desk," which contained hundreds of pigeonholes and could be closed and locked, allowing for the secure storage and access of personal work documents. The gradual development and innovation that led to vertical filing – a technology, perhaps unsurprisingly, developed by the inventor of the Dewey Decimal System – was a result of a data glut that began a century before anyone uttered the word "internet" (Yates 1982).

While subject-oriented classification made sense for the broad and relatively slowly changing materials of a library, it would have been useless when applied to the office of the last century. First, time was very much of the essence: *when* a document or file was created, changed, moved, or destroyed was often as important as the document's subject matter. Likewise, such records were often closely related to the people involved. Clearly this was true of customer records, and large insurance companies – whose very survival rested on increasing the size of their customer base – often drove innovations in business filing, right through to adopting the earliest electronic computers.

The earliest computer systems drew on the ideas of librarians and filing clerks, but were also constrained by the technology itself. While these earlier approaches provided metaphors for digital storage, they failed to consider the hardware constraints posed by the new computing devices and placed limits on the new capabilities of these machines. Computer programmers made use of queues and stacks of data, created new forms of encoding data digitally, and new imaginary structures for holding that data. Not housed in drawers or on shelves, these collections could be rearranged and cross-indexed much more quickly than their physical counterparts. Over time, this evolved into its own art, and database design continues to be a rapidly advancing subfield of computer science.

As the internet began its exponential increase in size during the 1990s, driven by the emergence of the World Wide Web, it became apparent that there was more information than could easily be browsed. What began as the equivalent of a personal office, with a small private library and a couple of filing cabinets, grew to rival and exceed the size of the largest libraries in the world. The change was not immediate, and, in the early stages, individuals were able to create guides that listed individual collections at various institutions, generally consisting of freely available software and a handful of large documents. Especially with the advent of the web, the physical machine where the documents were stored began to matter less and less, and the number of people contributing documents grew quickly. No longer could a person browse the web as if it were a small book shop, relatively confident that they had visited each and every shelf. Competing metaphors from librarians, organizational communicators, and computer programmers sought out ways of bringing order, but the search engine, in many ways, was a novel solution for this new information environment.

How a search engine works

Although the search engine has evolved considerably over time, all search engines share a common overall structure and function. Before outlining their development and commercialization over time, it is useful to understand how a basic search engine works. Our interaction with search engines, as users, is fairly uncomplicated. A website presents a box in which we type a few words we presume are relevant, and the engine produces a list of pages that contain that combination of words. In practice, this interface with the person, while important, is only one of three parts of what makes up a search engine. The production of the database queried by the web form requires, first, that information about webpages be gathered from around the web, and, second, that this collection of data be processed in such a way that a page's relevance to a particular set of keywords may be determined. By understanding the basic operation of each of these steps and the challenges they pose, an overall understanding of the technology may be reached. Figure 1.1 provides an overview of the process common to most search engines.

The process begins with a system that automatically calls up pages on the web and records them, usually called a *crawler*, *spider*, *web robot*, or *bot*. Imagine a person sitting at a computer browsing the web in a methodological way. She begins her process with a list of webpages she plans to visit. She types the

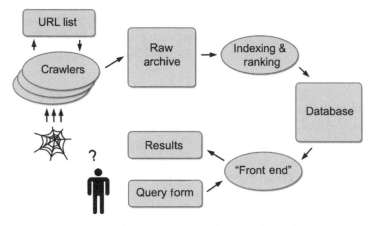

Figure 1.1. Conceptual organization of the typical search engine

URL for the first of these pages into the browser. Once it loads, she saves a copy of the page on her hard drive, noting the time and the date. She then looks through the page for any hyperlinks to other pages. If she finds hyperlinks that are not already on her list, she adds them to the bottom of the list. Following this pattern, she is likely to record a large part of the entire web. Once complete, she would begin again from the top of her list, as there are likely new pages that have been created and linked to since she began.

If the search engines really relied on individual humans to do this, it would take thousands of years to complete even a single crawl of the web. However, the operation described is not particularly complex, and creating a computer program that can duplicate this behavior is not difficult. Because the crawler is a relatively simple piece of technology, it has not evolved as much as other parts of the search engine. Even the smallest-scale crawlers are usually multi-threaded, making many requests at the same time rather than waiting for each page to be produced before moving on. They generally run not on a single computer, but on a large number of computers working in tandem. Most are careful to distribute their requests across the web, rather than ask for all of the pages from one server at once, since the crush of requests could easily overwhelm a single server, and most are "polite," taking into account webpage authors' requests for certain pages to be ignored.

That does not mean that crawlers are all the same. There is an entire menagerie of crawlers out looking for new content on the web. On many pages, visits by web robots outnumber visits by real people. Some of these – going by exotic names like Slurp and Teoma – are gathering information for the largest general-purpose search engines, but others may be run just once by an individual. Small crawlers are built into a number of applications, including plug-ins for browsers and a robot used by Adobe Acrobat to create a PDF from a web-site. Because of small differences in how they are pro-grammed, they behave slightly differently, following some links and not others, or coming back to re-check more or less frequently. There are a number of people who are trying to figure out just how these robots work so that they can ensure their message is presented to as many search engines as pos-sible (Valentine 2005).

However, following hyperlinks may not be enough. Large portions of the web are now generated dynamically, according to various requests from website visitors. Think, for example, of an online site that provides theater tickets. The calendar, the pages describing available tickets, or even the seating maps may change depending on the show, the location of the person accessing the site, the current date, previous sales, and other variables. Because these are not static, hyperlinked pages, they are not easily accessed by most crawlers, and are part of what is sometimes called the "deep web" beyond the reach of most search engines (Sherman & Price 2001). There are substantial technological and potential legal barriers to accessing this hidden web, but there continue to be efforts to create smarter crawlers able to index dynamic pages (Ntoulas, Zerfos, & Cho 2005). This is particularly true for search engines that are focused on ferreting out the best price among competing providers: finding the least expensive airfares for a given route, for example.

Most crawlers make an archival copy of some or all of a web-page, and extract the links immediately to find more pages to crawl. Some crawlers, like the Heritrix spider employed by the Internet Archive, the "wget" program often distributed with Linux, and web robots built into browsers and other web clients, are pretty much done at this stage. However, most crawlers create an archive that is designed to be parsed and organized in some way. Some of this processing (like "scraping" out links, or storing metadata) can occur within the crawler itself, but there is usually some form of processing of the text and code of a webpage afterward to try to obtain structural information about it.

The most basic form of processing, common to almost every modern search engine, is extraction of key terms to create a keyword index for the web by an "indexer." We are all familiar with how the index of a book works: it takes information about which words appear on any given page and reverses it so that you may learn which pages contain any given word. In retrospect, a full-text index of the web is one of the obvious choices for finding material online, but particularly in the early development of search engines it was not clear what parts should be indexed: the page titles, metadata, hyperlink text, or full text (Yuwono et al. 1995). If indexing the full text of a page, is it possible to determine which words are most important?

In practice, even deciding what constitutes a "word" (or a "term") can be difficult. For most western languages, it is possible to look for words by finding letters between the spaces and punctuation, though this becomes more difficult in languages like Chinese and Japanese, which have no clear markings between terms. In English, contractions and abbreviations cause problems. Some spaces mean more than others; someone looking for information about "York" probably has little use for pages that mention "New York," for instance. A handful of words like "the" and "my" are often dismissed as "stop words" and not included in the index because they are so common. Further application of natural language processing (NLP) is capable of determining the parts of speech of terms, and synonyms can be identified to provide further clues for searching. At the most extreme end of indexing are efforts to allow a computer to in some way understand the genre or topic of a given page by "reading" the text to determine its meaning.[1]

An index works well for a book. Even in a fairly lengthy work, it is not difficult to check each occurrence of a keyword, but the same is not true of the web. Generally, an exhaustive examination of each of the pages containing a particular keyword is impossible, particularly when much of the material is not just unhelpful, but – as in the case of spam – intentionally misleading. This is why results must be ranked according to perceived relevance, and the process by which a particular search engine indexes its content and ranks the results is really a large part of what makes it unique. One of the ways Google leapt ahead of its competitors early on is that it developed an algorithm called PageRank that relied on hyperlinks to infer the authority of various pages containing a given keyword. Some of the problems of PageRank will be examined in chapter 4. Here, it is enough to note that the process by which an index is established, and the attributes that are tracked, make up a large part of the "secret recipes" of the various search engines.

The crawling of the web and processing of that content happens behind the scenes, and results in a database of indexed material that may then be queried by an individual. The final piece of a search engine is its most visible part: the interface, or "front end," that accepts a query, processes it, and presents the results. The presentation of an initial request can be, and often is, very simple: the search box found in the corner of a webpage, for example. The sparse home page for the Google search engine epitomizes this simplicity. However, providing people with an extensive set of tools to tailor their search, and to refine their search, can lead to interesting challenges, particularly for large search engines with an extremely diverse set of potential users.

In some ways, the ideal interface anticipates people's behaviors, understanding what they expect and helping to reveal possibilities without overwhelming them. This can be done in a number of ways. Clearly the static design of the user interface is important, as is the process, or flow, of a search request. Westlaw, among other search engines, provides a thesaurus function to help users build more comprehensive searches. Search engines like Yahoo have experimented with auto-completing searches, anticipating what the person might be trying to type in the search box, and providing suggestions in real time (Calore 2007). It is not clear how effective these particular elements are, but they exemplify the aims of a good interface: a design that meets the user half-way.

Once a set of results are created, they are usually ranked in some way to provide a list of topics that present the most significant "hits" first. The most common way of displaying results is as a simple list, with some form of summary of each page. Often the keywords are presented in the context of the surrounding text. In some cases, there are options to limit or expand the search, to change the search terms, or to alter the search in some other way. More recently, some search engines provide results in categories, or mapped graphically.

All of these elements work together to keep a search engine continuously updated. The largest search engines are constantly under development to better analyze and present searchable databases of the public web. Some of this work is aimed at making search more efficient and useful, but some is required just to keep pace. The technologies used on the web change frequently, and, when they do, search engines have to change with them. As people employ Adobe Acrobat or Flash, search engines need to create tools to make sense of these formats. The sheer amount of material that must be indexed increases exponentially each year, requiring substantial investments in computing hardware and bandwidth. Someone visiting a skyscraper can quickly appreciate the work that went into building it, but few are aware of the work that must be continually done to make a search engine function.

Pre-web internet search

Once one has used a search engine, it seems obvious that it should exist, but the need for a general search engine during the early days of the web was neither immediate nor apparent. It usually is not until a collection of data grows too large to map in its entirety that the need for a search interface is made clear. Consider the average home library, which may fill only a bookcase or two. The books may be placed randomly, or by size, or by which are used more often or more appreciated, or by some idiosyncratic subject arrangement. At some point, however, a library grows to the point at which looking through everything to find the book you want is impractical, and at that point some form of indexing is necessary. Likewise, networked information started out as relatively small collections in relatively few repositories, and it was not until later that the need for different forms of indexing was made clear, and tools were created to meet this need.

Early technologies used for finding files or users were often built into the operating system and, once computers were networked, it was often possible to use the same functions from a distance. Since long before the web has existed, the Unix command "finger," for example, has provided information about a particular user, including when that user last logged on, and often some personal contact information. Its creator, Les Earnest, designed "finger" to aid in social networking at the Stanford Artificial Intelligence Lab (quoted in Shah 2000):

> People generally worked long hours there, often with unpredictable schedules. When you wanted to meet with some group, it was important to know who was there and when the others would likely reappear. It also was important to be able

to locate potential volleyball players when you wanted to play, Chinese food freaks when you wanted to eat, and antisocial computer users when it appeared that something strange was happening on the system.

When computers were networked via the internet, it was possible to "finger" individuals from across the country or the world, to find out more about them. Eventually, it was used for other purposes, including distributing weather reports.

The first indexes on the internet were created by hand, often by the users of the systems as a guide to others. Consider some of the protocols in use on the internet before the emergence of the World Wide Web, beginning with File Transfer Protocol (FTP), one of the first ways of moving files between computers. An early internet user would choose an FTP server from a list of public servers (a list they or someone else likely had downloaded from one of the servers on that list), and request a listing of files on that server. Often, there was a text document that could be downloaded that briefly summarized the content of each of the files on a given server. FTP continues to be used today as a way of transferring files, but the process of browsing through FTP servers in the hope of finding the document you were seeking was laborious and inconsistent, especially as the number of FTP servers increased. This increase also brought with it the rise of "anonymous" FTP servers, which allowed anyone to upload and download files to and from the server. While the increase in content was a boon to those who used the internet, it became increasingly difficult to locate specific files.

As a result, what might be considered the first search engine on the internet arrived in 1990, before the World Wide Web had gained a foothold, and at a time when many universities had only recently become a part of the network (P. Deutsch 2000). This system, called Archie, periodically visited the existing FTP sites and indexed their directories. It is probably a stretch to say that it "crawled" these sites, since unlike today's web crawlers it did not discover new servers linked to the existing servers. It also did not examine the full content of each of these pages, but limited itself to the titles of the files. Nonetheless, it represented a first effort to reign in a quickly growing, chaotic information resource, not by imposing order on it from above, but by mapping and indexing the disorder to make it more usable.

The Gopher system was another attempt to bring order to the early internet. It made browsing files more practical, and represented an intermediary step in the direction of the World Wide Web. People could navigate through menus that organized documents and other files, and made it easier, in theory, to find what you might be looking for. Gopher lacked hypertext – you could not indicate a link and have that link automatically load another document in quite the same way it can be done on the web – but it facilitated working through directory structures, and insulated the individual from a command-line interface. Veronica, named after Archie's girlfriend in 1940s-era comics, was created to provide a broader index of content available on Gopher servers. Like Archie, it provided the capability of searching titles (actually, menu items), rather than the full text of the documents available, but it required a system that could crawl through the menu-structured directories of "gopherspace" to discover each of the files (Parker 1994).

In 1991, the World Wide Web first became available, and with the popularization of a graphical browser, Mosaic, in 1993, it began to grow even more quickly. The most useful tool for the web user of the early 1990s was a good bookmark file, a collection of URLs that the person had found to be useful. People began publishing their bookmark files to the web as pages, and this small gesture has had an enormous impact on how we use the web today. The collaborative filtering and tagging sites that are popular today descended from this practice, and the updating and annotating of links to interesting new websites led to some of the first proto-blogs. Most importantly, it gave rise to the first collaborative directories and search engines.

The first of these search engines, Wandex, was developed by Matthew Grey at the Massachusetts Institute of Technology, and was based on the files gathered by his crawler, the World Wide Web Wanderer. It was, again, developed to fulfill a particular need. The web was made for browsing, but perhaps to an even greater degree than FTP and Gopher, it had no overarching structure that would allow people to locate documents easily. Many attribute the genesis of the idea of the web to an article that had appeared just after the Second World War entitled "As we may think", in which Vannevar Bush (1945) suggests that a future global encyclopedia will allow individuals to follow "associative trails" between documents. In practice, the web grows in a haphazard fashion, like a library that consists of a pile of books that grows as anyone throws anything they wish onto the pile. A large part of what an index needed to do was to discover these new documents and make sense of them. Perhaps more than any previous collection, the web cried out for indexing, and that is what Wandex did.

As with Veronica, the Wanderer had to work out a way to follow hyperlinks and crawl this new information resource, and, like its predecessors, it limited itself to indexing titles. Brian Pinkerton's WebCrawler, developed in 1994, was one of the first web-available search engines (along with the Repository-Based Software Engineering ["RBSE"] spider and indexer; see Eichmann 1994) to index the content of these pages. This was important, Pinkerton suggested, because titles provided little for the individual to go on; in fact, a fifth of the pages on the web had no titles at all (Pinkerton 1994). Receiving its millionth query near the end of 1994, it clearly had found an audience on the early web, and, by the end of 1994, more than a half-dozen search engines were indexing the web.

Searching the web

Throughout the 1990s, advances in search engine technology were largely incremental, with a few exceptions. Generally, the competitive advantage of one search engine or another had more to do with the comparative size of its database, and how quickly that database was updated. The size of the web and its phenomenal growth were the most daunting technical challenge any search engine designer would have to face. But there were some advances that had a significant impact. A number of search engines, including SavvySearch, provided metasearch: the ability to query multiple search engines at once (A.E. Howe & Dreilinger 1997). Several, particularly Northern Light, included material under license as part of their search results, extending access beyond what early web authors were willing to release broadly (and without charge) to the web. Northern Light was also one of the first to experiment with clustering results by topic, something that many search engines are now continuing to develop. Ask Jeeves attempted to make the query process more user-friendly and intuitive, encouraging people to ask fully formed questions rather than use Boolean search queries, and AltaVista provided some early ability to refine results from a search.

One of the greatest challenges search engines had to face, particularly in the late 1990s, was not just the size of the web, but the rapid growth of spam and other attempts to manipulate search engines in an attempt to draw the attention of a larger audience. A later chapter will address this game of cat-and-mouse in more detail, but it is worth noting here that it represented a significant technical obstacle and resulted in a perhaps unintended advantage for Google, which began providing search functionality in 1998. It took some time for those wishing to manipulate search engines to understand how Google's reliance on hyperlinks as a measure of reputation worked, and to develop strategies to influence it.

At the same time, a number of directories presented a complementary paradigm for organizing the internet. Yahoo, LookSmart, and others, by using a categorization of the internet, gave their searches a much smaller scope to begin with. The Open Directory Project, by releasing its volunteer-edited, collaborative categorization, provided another way of mapping the space. Each of these provided the ability to search, in addition to browsing their directory structures. Since the indexed material had already been selected, often by hand, as being of general interest or utility, searches on these sites could be very effective. Eventually many of these directory-based portals became major players, particularly Yahoo, who experimented with a number of search engine partnerships, beginning with combining Inktomi's search technology with their existing directory in 1998, and eventually acquiring some of the largest general-purpose search engines, including AlltheWeb.com, AltaVista, and HotBot.

The early development of search engines was largely centered in the United States. By the middle of the 1990s, the World Wide Web was beginning to live up to its name, and sites could be found in many parts of the world, but American sites in English continued to make up the bulk of the web. Around the mid-1990s, the number of web users and websites exploded in Europe, as well as Hong Kong, New Zealand, and other countries. Unsurprisingly, even though the United States hosted the most websites, sites outside of the USA tended not to link "Worldwide," but rather to other sites hosted in the same country, or back to the core of sites in the United States (Halavais 2000). Likewise, users in these countries tended to purchase items from local merchants rather than take advantage of the global web-based marketplace (Jupiter Communications 1999). Just as search engine competition was heating up in the United States, many around the world were asking why they should use a search engine that was not suited to their own culture and language. In this, the World Wide Web tended to reinscribe existing flows of global information, even as it presented some alternatives.

The rise of regional search engines is often left out of the history of search, but, by the mid-1990s, many countries and linguistic groups were relying on services tailored to their own languages and interests. Early examples included the Swiss search.ch, an Israeli engine called Walla, France's Voilà, and the Russian Rambler. More recently, non-English-language search is again in the news, with the Chinese Baidu attracting a strong global following (in several languages) and the French government encouraging the development of francophone search.

There can be little doubt that, by the late 2000s, search engines are ascendant. While the phrase "surfing the internet" remains, the dominant paradigm is no longer moving from site to site in a sea of hyperlinks, but rather searching for specific items, or browsing through particular guides. More than a decade ago, Jacques Altaber, an official at CERN (Conseil Européen pour la Recherche Nucléaire), the organization that first supported the World Wide Web, suggested that the web would become a new sort of operating system, the platform on which an ever greater proportion of our communication and information tasks take place (James 1995). In the space of fifteen years, search engines have become central to that operating system, moving from a useful tool to a powerful focal point of collective attention.

Many of those who initially developed search engines did so because they had a need and answered it. Many successful search engines were designed by students, and some of those pioneers now work in what has become a substantial search engine industry. The author of Wandex, for example, now works for Google, and the creator of the original WebCrawler works for Technorati, each improving on the technology of search. But WebCrawler is emblematic in another way. It was developed in 1993, a year that was important because it marked the commercialization of the World Wide Web, and, with it, the search engine. By 1994, WebCrawler had two commercial advertisers sponsoring the site, and, in the middle of 1995, it had been acquired by America Online as part of their effort to bridge to the web. The story of the development of the search engine is tied inextricably to the commercialization of the online world, and although there continue to be a number of important search engines that are supported by government or research funding, the search engine wars of the 2000s were driven by the potential profit of online advertising.

The rise of the search engine coincided with the dot-com bubble, especially during the late 1990s, and large sums were invested in developing new and existing search engines and competing for a share of the search engine market. Over time, many of these search engines were acquired by their competitors, and the field narrowed somewhat. By the early 2000s, Google had come onto the scene and rapidly seized a large proportion of the global search market. At present, Google remains the most popular destination for those who are looking for a search engine. Microsoft began offering MSN Search in 2005, and more recently has launched a new effort squarely aimed at Google, called Live. Yahoo Search and Ask remain active competitors in the search market, a market that is driven by innovation, and new challenges come from engines like Hakia and Mahalo and dozens of others being developed around the world.

Vertical search

Unlike many other technologies that move from small-scale to large-scale implementation, search engines have recently moved from general web-wide search to the ability to search smaller site- and topic-specific domains. Country- and language-specific search is now thriving. While the large search engines attempt to "organize the world's information" (as Google says), a few countries were left behind. Particular languages that made use of non-roman character sets were ill served by existing search engines. Languages that make use of diacritic marks found that searches might bring up items that were clearly not related to their own interests by failing to distinguish words that might appear to be similar without the marks. The difficulty was particularly pronounced in Asian countries, where even tokenization – separating words from one another by looking for spaces – was complicated by the nature of the language. One size of search engine clearly did not fit all. Especially with the growth of the Chinese-language internet, search engines like

Baidu appear to represent not a niche, but a very substantial segment of the world market.

Aside from linguistically or culturally relevant search engines, niches of every type are gaining their own search tools. The Bioinformatic Harvester, for example, potentially has a global, multi-lingual audience that is widely dispersed, but with a rather narrow interest in searching genetic materials (Liebel, Kindler, & Pepperkok 2005). There are much larger verticals in product search, job search, and search for medical information. Given the need for domain knowledge and sometimes content agreements required to develop some of these vertical search engines, it seems very likely that there will continue to be innovation within particular niches. Many of these efforts are acquired by the large search engines when they become successful, with the aims of both financial and technological integration with other verticals.

Google and Yahoo have well-established country-specific domains (e.g. yahoo.co.jp) that service non-English-language searchers, and while they often compete with locally created alternatives – either in the form of search engines or in the form of directories – the integration with existing infrastructure provides them with some advantage. The major players have been eager to move into new areas, including geospatial search, mobile devices, and the like. The largest companies are also best poised to engage in capital-intensive verticals, like Google's efforts to digitize several university libraries to open up their printed material to full-text web search. Using search as the foundation, search engines have moved into other services, including email, word processing, and mobile telephony. If the web is becoming a globally distributed operating system, search engine companies have a substantial degree of leverage in connecting people to software tools and content.

Much of the battle for search supremacy consists of small and large search engine developers vying to provide the search function for corporate intranets. For Google, who has seen its sales to enterprise customers double each year for the last several years, being a dominant force among public search engines provides the advantage not only of name recognition, but also of a chance to test new products on a large number of users – products that can later be sold at the enterprise level (Hines 2007). It is clear that advertising will remain the bedrock for financing most search on the web, but enterprise search, and the services that can be integrated with it, remain an important part of many search engine companies' financial health.

As the content reached by search engines is expanded, so too are the ways in which search is being developed. Some of these approaches have a long history of experimentation and need only fine tuning. Clustering search results by topic, for example, has been a long-term project that is now seeing wider adoption by several search engines, and some of these are providing graphical representations of the clusters. The semantic web – an evolutionary step that would allow for more structured exchange of data over the web – has yielded its own experimental forms of search. NLP approaches are being used to better understand text on the web and individuals' queries. The use of human coding, either implicit or explicit, is increasingly a core part of many approaches to what has come to be known as "social search." In all, while both the technology and the industry went through a period of consolidation early in the decade, and despite the current dominance of Google, there are now a number of new ways search engines are evolving in terms of technology and their relationship to the larger media industry. The way society uses search engines, and is changed by that use, is also rapidly evolving.

Social search engines?

Search engines were developed as a response to a particular social problem, a problem that did not exist in the same way in the past. The signature technology of the last few decades has been digitization: the ability to transfer communications media into a format that may be transmitted via computer networks. As a result, more information is available in more places than ever before. This embarrassment of riches has necessitated new ways of filtering, sorting, and finding information. This is an old story – necessity as the mother of invention – and it is tempting to leave it at that. Indeed, the technical problems are challenging and exciting.

It would be wrong to assume, however, that the social and cultural needs that led to the creation of search engines no longer are of import. Perhaps more than ever, our evolving ideas of what a search engine should do shape its development, either by creating new needs (finding video content, for example), or in some cases by resisting change in favor of familiarity. It is important, if we want to understand the technology better, to understand the social and informational environments in which it is deployed.

Understanding how people use search engines can also give us a seemingly unobtrusive way of learning about society's interests in the aggregate. Encouraged in part by Google's Zeitgeist pages, which provide an indication of search terms that have become suddenly more popular in a given week, John Battelle (2005) considers search engines to be a source of a sort of global "database of intentions," providing what could ultimately become a fine-grained map of our interests and personalities as individuals and groups. In other words, by learning how people behave when using search engines, we may come to understand how they behave in general.

Perhaps the most intriguing question is how search engines have changed us. Battelle's suggestion is that measuring intentions through the search engine is especially accurate because, unlike surveys or other methods of measuring public and private opinion, it directly infers intent by measuring behavior online. But it seems unlikely that those behaviors have not been changed significantly by the use of a search engine. No new technology leaves us unchanged, and often the changes are unexpected and unpredictable. More than two millennia ago, Plato was already making the case that communication technologies changed who we were, and not always for the better. Rather than enhancing memory, he argues in the *Phaedrus* (2002), writing subsumes it, and reduces the abilities of those who read rather than remember. This double edge of technology – and particularly of communication technology, since communication is at the core of our social interactions – represents one of the most pressing reasons we must examine the role of the search engine not just *in* society, but in permeating our social lives. The following chapter examines how we use search engines, and how they have, in turn, changed us as a society.

CHAPTER TWO

Searching

There are at least three questions we can ask about the search process. The first of these deals with the concrete issue of how people enter items into a search engine query box and how they interpret the results. This interaction at the interface level is of particular interest to the designers of search engines, and tells us a lot about search engines, the people who use them, and how we all think about our world. The broader question is *why* people search, what motivates them to look for certain material on a search engine, and whether they are in some way satisfied by what they find. Finally, we might ask whether the mere existence of a search engine changes what people *want* to look for, and their social values and expectations. That is, do the motivations surrounding search change with the existence of particular search engines?

A more complete understanding of the search engine requires that we look at search from a variety of perspectives. The perspective of the "user" is an obvious starting point – or at least one would imagine so. The creation of software is undergoing a small revolution that is sometimes called "user-centered design" (Vredenburg, Isensee, & Righi 2001). Rather than trusting designers' innate understanding of the problem of the search process, and their internalized models of who might be using their system, user-centered design requires an iterative process of understanding what the user expects and creating systems that help to satisfy users' needs and desires.

There are problems with this approach, one of which is assuming that users do not also change to adapt to systems. Douglas Engelbart, who may be considered the father of the user interface, has long argued that information systems and users co-evolve (Engelbart & Lehtman 1988). His work at Stanford, which brought about the mouse, hyperlinking, word processing, and dozens of other elements of the modern interface that we now take for granted, was oriented toward tools that would augment "the capability of humans to deal with tough knowledge work and to process effectively the large volumes of information with which knowledge workers must deal." He suggested that as a community became accustomed to particular interfaces, they created new needs. This means that there is no possibility for some sort of a "perfect interface," any more than there is a "perfect search engine." New online services lead to new capabilities among the user base, and new desires to be fulfilled. It is not enough to react to the user, or create systems that respond to existing needs; the designer must understand the current user, and at the same time anticipate how the system might change the user.

Search engine literacy

Even if the perfect interface does not exist in real life, it persists in our dreams. This dream interface usually comes in two forms. One form is represented by the holographic artificially intelligent librarian, named Vox, from the 2002 version of the film *Time Machine*. Library users are able to interact with Vox as they might with an omniscient research librarian. He takes into consideration their age and experience, is able to summarize resources in natural speech, can interpret the gestures of the user (pointing to an artifact, for example, or looking confused), and can be redirected by the user when he is proceeding in a direction different from what the user intends. Unfortunately, even this sort of ideal of a search engine as an embodied intelligent agent is not perfect. Our interactions with humans can be at least as frustrating as our interactions with machines.

Perhaps, then, the ideal device is one that knows what you mean: a perfect interface with your brain, an interface that knows what you are thinking (Hansell 2007). This is hardly a new dream. The ability to communicate to another person exactly what you mean has been an objective of just about every philosophy of every culture. Umberto Eco, in his *Search for the perfect language* (1995), recounts some of these attempts, from recovering lost "original languages," to constructing logical grammars for philosophy or model universal languages. There is some of this dream of a philosophical language in current efforts toward the construction of ontologies and the "semantic web." This is not the first time new technologies were considered the gateway to "angelic speech," or mind-to-mind communication. The radio, for example, was seen as a way to link up minds so that a new global understanding might be reached (J. D. Peters 1999). A functioning semantic web would change the way we think about search engines, since the problem would no longer be one of inferring whether a page matched the needs of a query, but rather of forming the query itself. In other words, the problem would likely be shifted to the interface with users, and users' abilities to understand the structures of knowledge being used. The ideal interface requires no such translation; it knows just what you mean.

The difficulty is that the searcher does not always know precisely what she means; if she did, she would have little need of searching. The word "search" suggests that a person is interested in finding something that has been lost. People do use search engines for this, particularly to "re-find" information that they may already have encountered on the web, but more often they are hoping not to "find" but to "learn," or to "discover." Perhaps, then, the ideal search engine does not just understand what you desire, but knows what the user wants even when she does not know herself. That is a conundrum, but may not be an insurmountable challenge.

The greater obstacle is the diversity of knowledge, skills, and abilities of users who come to the search engine. Accessing the web is now easier than ever, although it is certainly easier for some than it is for others. Even as the network continues to reach out across the globe, a second-level digital divide becomes clearer between those who are skilled users of the internet and those who are not. We already know that different people have different aptitudes when it comes to searching the web, and so it is a more useful resource to some than it is to others (Hargittai 2002a).

Searching skills

It is commonly believed that searching requires no skill at all, and too easy to assume that "digital natives," those who grew up with web access throughout their childhood, have had enough exposure to search engines to have natural expertise. While young people may not remember a time before search engines, that does not mean that they are particularly adept at using them (Heine 2007). Some of the things many of us now do without thinking had to be learned at some point, and because these behaviors are so ingrained, we fail to remember that they are not part of the average seeker's collection of skills.

There are really two dangers here. The first is assuming that, because these "digital natives" are members of a generation that has been immersed in digital networking, they represent the cutting edge of its use. This would suggest that those who have different schema for seeking, for example, academic information are merely behind the times. The other mistake, perhaps unsurprisingly the one made by experienced librarians and scholars, is to assume that the web and search engines are always less appropriate tools for finding reliable information. It does not take much to notice that college students today are likely to turn to a large search engine to make initial inquiries on academic topics, rather than to the library catalog or databases. By 2001, more than 90 percent of American teenagers turned to the web to help them to complete assignments (Lenhart, Simon, & Graziano 2001). This can cause a significant disconnect between those who have traditionally been guardians of knowledge and new students.

In practice, students use the internet because it is convenient, and because it often provides them with current information in a format that is easily accessible. They are more likely to
do this in their homes than in school, either because access at
school is more difficult, or because they have more freedom
to discover on their own at home (Levin & Arafeh 2002).
Unfortunately, despite the popularity of using search engines
to find school-related information on the web – by 2005, on any
given day 56 percent of American internet users had looked up
something on a search engine – students may have more confidence in their ability to find and evaluate information than is
warranted. In one survey, for example, while 92 percent of the
users were confident in their searching abilities, 62 percent
were unaware of any distinction between paid search results
and unpaid results (Fallows 2005). It makes sense that students
are using search engines more, and it is fair to expect that
searching information systems will be an important part of
their work experiences as they get older. For that reason, among
others, it is important to think about search engine use not just
as an auxiliary skill, but as an important part of a new digital literacy (Labbo, Reinking, & McKenna 1998).

Guinee, Eagleton, and Hall (2003) studied how secondary-
school students found information on the web. They categorize
the three most popular methods as the "dot-com formula," the
"shopping mall," and the "search engine." Despite the popularity of search engines, it is generally not the first place adolescents go when they are seeking to answer questions. Instead,
they often derive a topic, and then check to see if a relevant
domain exists. This makes sense for many sorts of queries: if
you want to know about a particular company, for example, it is
reasonably safe to assume that adding ".com" to the end of the
name might yield something useful. This is such a common
thought that many people enter domain names into search
engines – which in practice is quite redundant. Adolescents
who have a bit more experience with the web will often "shop"
sites that they are already aware of to look for particular

information. For example, for a question related to an actor, they might recognize that IMDB.com would be appropriate. Were the study repeated today, it would be surprising if Wikipedia were not among the most popular of "shopping sites" for finding basic information. With these strategies exhausted, students turn to a search engine. Experienced searchers among the students often had a favorite search engine.

The skill most likely to affect the success of a search is the ability to choose the appropriate keywords. How can you know which terms, or combination of terms, best targets the information you are after? To know how to choose the best search terms, you must understand how the search engine indexes the web, and pick terms that exploit this process. First, you must understand that search engines, at their core, represent an index of terms on the web; that, for the most part, they do not attempt to summarize pages, for example. Understanding search engines as indexes means that the searcher is able to create a mental model of a webpage that meets their needs, and then can pick the search terms that are likely to be present on that page.

The searcher is likely to be even better prepared if they know that most search engines look for words, and sometimes phrases, that distinguish the page from other pages; that is, particularly uncommon phrases. Finding a single uncommon term is not an easy prospect. There are a limited number of terms in any language. English is particularly rich in this regard, and the second edition of the *Oxford English Dictionary* contains just over 228,000 words, to which you must add hundreds of thousands of technical terms, borrowed terms from Latin and other languages, and proper nouns. In short, English alone probably contains several million potential search terms. But the web contains at least several billion pages, each of them with a collection of these words. It is clear that the word "the" is of no use at all in answering any sort of specific question. Short, common words like "the" or "to" are generally considered "stop words" and ignored by search engines precisely because they are so useless.

In addition, most search engines look for words that "matter." If you look at the index at the end of this book, you will find that it does not contain most of the words on this page. The author and publisher have selected words they think are most distinctive of a discussion, and excluded words like "excluded," because they are so general as to be useless. Search engines actively exclude only a very small number of words, but some give added weight to terms and phrases that appear frequently on a given page, and comparatively less frequently on the rest of the web. This allows for the results to reflect pages that are less likely to mention a term "in passing." Even knowing this, however, single terms are unlikely to be particularly successful in returning useful results.

Marc Prensky (2004) suggests that "pretty much every Digital Native can program to some extent, even if it is only setting up and personalizing his or her cell phone, or using 'and' or 'or' in search engines." On the contrary, it is clear that while expert searchers use these Boolean operators and other constraints on their searches (Hogan 1998), the vast majority (at least 92 percent) of everyday searchers are unaware of these operators, let alone more specialized ways of tailoring a query. Nonetheless, it may be that, once again, we are applying presearch-engine experiences in information retrieval to a new system. In 2003, Bernard Jansen tested out the hypothesis that searchers would have more success when using complex queries, and determined that "the use of queries operators is generally not worth the trouble for the typical Web searcher."

One of the best ways of constraining a search is to use multiple search terms. As noted above, any English-language word is likely to show up on thousands, or even millions, of individual pages, but by combining even two words, a searcher can reduce the number of results significantly. Several years ago, a game emerged around this principle, called "Googlewhacking," in which the aim was to find two terms that appeared together on only a single page.[1] The difficulty of that task illustrates the reason for using multiple search terms.

On average, most people who enter a query on a search engine follow it up with another query or two, modifying their search in order to achieve a better result (Jansen, Spink, & Saracevic 2000). In many of these cases, the user is merely retyping the query, or adjusting spelling. In others, they realize that they need to provide a further restriction in order to narrow the results they have received. Someone searching for The The, a musical group that had some popularity in the 1980s, would realize after typing the name into a search engine that it was not a narrow enough search, and try *"The The" band*. This process of coming up with and expanding the keywords used to discover information is inevitably one of trial and error. Experienced searchers expect their searching to be iterative, refining keywords and engaging in focused browsing until the search goals are met (Hölscher & Strube 2000). In some cases, the search engine can help to refine the search in some way, or even suggest potential avenues for limiting the results.

Expert searchers recognize that search is not only an iterative process, but one that is rarely linear and requires seeking out the concepts that surround a problem or question (Webber 2002). In other words, the query and search strategy is likely to change as more information becomes available. That information is unlikely to come from a single "winning" source, but it is a result of gathering, evaluating, and comparing information from a range of sources. Bates (1989) has famously termed this approach to information seeking "berrypicking," and differentiates it from the classical model of information retrieval. Even basic information-seeking online is a complicated process, and since it is unlikely that a single interface is best able to provide support for the variety of types of searches and searchers, a diversity of different search engines and techniques is crucial.

Some searchers assume that when they use a search engine, especially when a search results in hundreds of thousands of pages, that the search engine has indexed the entire web. Many, however, recognize that search engines differ significantly in the amount of the web they have successfully indexed. At the peak of search engine innovation, Bharat and Broder (1998) found that only 1.4 percent of the pages managed to make it into all four of the most popular search engines; the rest were present on one or more of the engines, but not all. For those inexperienced with search, a single search on a large search engine may seem like enough. In fact, the same query on several search engines independently, or through a metasearch engine, can yield a wider range of results.

Even the most complete search engine is likely to have missed much of what is called the "invisible web" or "deep web." That might even be a good thing. As one group of early search engine pioneers noted, "It is safe to say that at least 99% of the available data is of no interest to at least 99% of the users" (Bowman et al. 1994), and, as a result, a general-purpose search engine probably does not need to index the entirety of the web at once. Some estimate that fully 80 percent of the content on the web is hidden from the general-purpose horizontal search engines (Ratzan 2006), while others suggest that proportion is much, much larger, estimating that, for every page in a major search engine's index, there are 500 missing (Sullivan 2000). Especially if the latter estimate remains true today, the sheer size and rate of growth of the web is enough to suggest why search engines have an incomplete index, but there are several other reasons, as well.

The search engine's crawler must usually be able to follow a hyperlink to arrive at and index a page; if the page is not hyperlinked from another HTML page somewhere on the web, it is unlikely to be indexed. Anything other than HTML – including document formats (Adobe Acrobat or Microsoft Word, for example), Shockwave and other executable files, archived ("zipped") files, video, and audio – presents a novel challenge to a search engine, and that challenge is even greater when there are hyperlinks within those documents. Things like live feeds, links to virtual worlds,[2] or even robots that can be controlled from the web (see, e.g., Schulz et al. 2000), are very difficult to anticipate and make sense of in the context of search. Much of the material available through the web can only be accessed through local searches on individual sites. Consider, for example, all of the pages available from a public library's web portal. There is probably a page for each book available in the library, but these pages probably do not appear as results from a search on a general-purpose site.

Finally, a large proportion of the web is explicitly excluded from web crawlers. This can occur in three ways. Many websites require a username and password to view some or all of their content. Sometimes this login information is even free of charge, but general-purpose search engines are unable to obtain an account. Some sites employ the robot exclusion protocol, which explicitly instructs search engine crawlers to ignore some or all of the pages on a site. Finally, some pages present different information depending on the location of the viewer. By noting the IP address of the visitor, it can determine what country or city the visitor is coming from and change the language and content of the site accordingly.

Expert searchers know about the hidden web, and know – at least within particular domains – how to access it. This approach brings back the "shopping mall" model, and requires familiarity with specialist search engines and directories. That familiarity is likely to come only with experience or focused exploration. If the average web surfer is looking for information on an individual, she is likely to key that person's name into a general-purpose search engine in the hope that something will come of it. With more experience, she might turn to search engines dedicated to the task (Zoominfo, Spock, or one of many others), search social networking sites like LinkedIn or Facebook, or check industry organization or company membership directories. The even more experienced might access proprietary networks and public records. While metasearch engines are drawing some of this material together, it is likely that the invisible web will be with us for some time to come (Sherman & Price 2001).

Throughout the search process, the user is likely to be evaluating results, allowing the nature of the search to evolve as more information is located. The precise strategy differs from searcher to searcher, but as most search engines provide some form of summary of the results, the evaluation begins there. Ironically, part of that evaluation stems from trust in the search engine itself. The mere fact that a search engine has suggested a site lends it credibility. Eye-tracking studies have shown that we are drawn to the top of the first page of results, and may ignore results that are lower on the page, let alone buried on subsequent results pages (Guan & Cutrell 2007). That trust extends to the sites themselves, and if a search engine leads a user to a page that is not at all relevant, many users – especially inexperienced users – will continue to browse that site, assuming they were sent there for a reason.

There is evidence that, although education is important, sophisticated search behaviors are most directly a result of practice: users with more experience with search are likely to be more sophisticated searchers (Howard & Massanari 2007). It is important to keep in mind that, even as search engine users are changing, there will likely always be not just a range of skill levels, but a diversity of approaches to search. Just as teachers are coming to understand that their classrooms are filled with students of not just differing abilities, but different orientations to the material, those interested in search need to recognize a spectrum of skills and approaches (Gardner 1983). As people become more experienced searchers, rather than approaching some idealized vision of a search engine user, they tend to adopt more complex and individualized approaches to the search activity.

A diversity of search

Researchers readily admit that searchers on the web are probably more diverse in background and in intent when compared with users of early information retrieval systems

(Jansen, Spink, & Saracevic 2000), but the prototypical search experience is still thought of as academic, in part because that is what those designing information retrieval systems are most familiar with. As a practical matter, searching for material in order to write a paper represents a fairly specific, and relatively infrequent, use of search engines. Andrei Broder (2002) has suggested that, in addition to the traditional informational searches, searches may also be navigational (e.g. wanting to find a site with music reviews) or transactional (e.g. finding where to buy a cheap moped). Though some work has been done to try to understand the relationship between concepts and the choice of keywords, this is likely to be different when looking for an academic source than it is for many other contexts.

Consider a specific example: just before a long trip, a colleague's daughter managed to get her head stuck in a toilet training seat, and he had to try to figure out how to free her. Rather than turning to relatives or a doctor, he did what many would in recent years: he turned to a search engine. A quick search for *potty seat head stuck* yielded a number of results, including instructional videos, and several suggestions for removing the seat. This and other minor emergencies are averted on a daily basis thanks to both the production of diverse amateur content for the web, and the ability to find it. The web tells us how to do things. Finding this information is often as easy as searching for the process you wish to learn about – like *replace shower fixture* – and most web users have sought such information on the web (Madden 2005).

Many searches are related to planned action: for example, deciding where to travel, whether a restaurant is good, if it is a good idea to use a particular method of organizing an office, or which automobile to buy. This sort of information gathering in support of a decision is a very common use of the web. The process is likely to involve not seeking an exact solution to a problem, but rather gathering a set of sources and information that can then be evaluated and analyzed by the searcher.

Decomposing a complex search problem into its constituent elements and analytically mining the web represents what we commonly think of as "critical thinking," and search patterns may represent this. But many effective searches also bring in more intuitive approaches that reflect pressures of time and attention common to every search task, and the expertise brought by experience (Klein 1999).

Sometimes the specific information needed is related to the context in which the information is being sought. Someone interested in the locations of car washes in the aggregate sense is very different from someone in their car, on a particular street, looking for the nearest car wash that is able to shampoo their rugs. In the latter case, it would be helpful if the search engine understood where you are, and that you are using a mobile device with a small screen, when guiding your search.

Researchers have recently become interested in the process of "re-finding" information that had been sought out and discovered in the past (Capra & Pérez-Quiñones 2005; Aula, Jhaveri, & Käki 2005). Search engines have often retained a history of an individual's searches, and sometimes provided that information to users, or, for privacy reasons, allowed them to delete the record. On the web, the traditional way of remembering a site was to bookmark it, but these bookmarks can become overwhelming to manage, and bookmarking systems like del.icio.us now allow for these reminders to be searched. If someone is able to remember enough about a particular page, it makes sense that they should be able to conduct a search that is very specific. As more and more of the world is in some way represented on the web, the process of remembering will also become linked to search in interesting ways. It might be valuable to think of "re-finding" not as a subset of finding, but the other way around. The search for new information may be profitably conceptualized as "re-finding" pages that you never encountered before. How is it that we model the page we are looking for, and how does our experience as a search engine user shape that model?

A related approach is ongoing, real-time search. For many individuals and companies, it is important to learn of new items on the web that meet their interests and needs. In these cases, it is not re-finding existing results, but reusing searches that have worked in the past. In these types of searches, and in many others, it can be helpful to search by similarity to previously discovered pages. On some search engines, a result may be followed by a link to find "more like this." Given the difficulty of interpreting the average searcher's queries, a great deal of research seeks new ways of finding conceptual similarity among documents, to allow for this sort of query-free searching.

The picture that emerges shows search to be a complex process, a process that becomes even more complex as the searchers become more adept. There remains a place for the simple search interface, and there seems little doubt that the largest search engines will continue to develop these. At present, the interfaces for expert searchers are less capable than they should be. By understanding expert searchers, and their needs for querying, extracting, recording, and recombining data iteratively, we may also better understand how to serve the less sophisticated searcher.

Tracking searches and searchers

One of the difficulties in modeling a perfect search strategy is that the search engines are, themselves, in a constant state of flux, and at least some of that flux is hidden. As we shall see in chapter 3, an industry has grown up around understanding just how search engines are operating at any given moment. At one point, when updates were less frequent, webmasters referred to the "Google dance," during which the latest iteration of Google's search algorithms would decide which pages would receive more privileged placement in search results.

At the same time, major search engines have continuously changed the way their systems worked in order to respond to pressures both from those who would seek to exploit the search engine to present their own pages in the best light, and from users who demand more accurate results even as the information environment becomes more complex. There is no ideal search strategy because search engine developers are trying to make the engine better fit how the user is already searching.

The problem is how to understand just what the user is doing. One of the first sources of such data is Transaction Log Analysis (TLA). Most interactions on the web are recorded in some way. When a person visits a website, that site records a set of information: usually the time of the visit, the user's IP address, some basic information about the user's browser and operating system, and what page referred the user to the current page. Search logs provide much of the same data, but also include information about what queries are entered. At a basic level that is all a log contains, but more information can be inferred from these individual entries. A path can be constructed that indicates attempted and successful searches, changes in keywords, and the like (Jansen & Pooch, 2000).

Simply looking at the queries that users generate can provide some information about how people search. This may be part of the reason that a ticker at Google headquarters shows real-time queries of the search engine on one wall. The first challenge to understanding these queries is the sheer volume of the data. One such early analysis, for example, attempted to make sense of half a billion queries on the AltaVista search engine (Silverstein et al. 1999). Faced with such a large number of queries and search sessions, it is difficult to even draw out statistical information about the types of query data, and perhaps the general topic area.

These transaction logs may be enhanced in a number of ways, many of which come under the umbrella term "web analytics." Most search engines now add a script to allow them to track which links the user clicks, allowing them to link queries to the results the user finds most interesting. This kind of tracking of implicit decisions is particularly important for search engines, as it is possible to infer the relevance of the produced results by seeing which items the user clicks through (Joachims et al. 2007).

The use of cookies provides even more extensive opportunities for tracking what users are doing when they search. Since Google provides a federated login to all of their services, it also means that they are able to track user behavior across applications. A large number of websites use Google Analytics, a free web analytics package, as well as advertising through AdWords, which presumably provides Google with even more information about what users are doing even when they are not visiting Google-branded sites. This sort of tracking by DoubleClick, the web advertising company, raised privacy concerns years ago. DoubleClick has recently been acquired by Google.

Although transaction logs, even in their most enhanced state, usually reside on the host machine, in some cases transactions are recorded on the client side. This can provide a much clearer picture of how a single user makes use of the web, and their strategies for finding information. Companies that provide ratings and traffic data often rely on client-side logs of representative (and sometimes not-so-representative) web users to determine which sites are particularly popular. Those client-side logs, when employed by researchers, provide the advantage of tracking exactly where users go on the internet, as they move from site to site. Many such logs provide even more detailed information, including recording keystrokes, mouse position, and the use of applications other than the web browser (Westerman et al. 1996; Arroyo, Selker, & Wei 2006).

Each of these approaches has the advantage of being relatively unobtrusive. In the case of server-side logs, most users do not even know they are being tracked, though recent well-publicized releases of search logs may change this awareness. It is reasonable to assume that users might behave in different ways when they recognize that they are being observed, and so this sort of analysis "in the wild" remains a particularly widely used source of information. While the information may be unbiased, it can be somewhat diffuse, and requires a great deal of inference if you are interested in users' intents.

Greater availability of eye-tracking hardware has provided a new tool for understanding how people interact with the search engine interface. Eye tracking allows the researcher to determine what elements of a page draw the searcher's attention, and in what order. Much of this work supports a concept called "information foraging," which argues that searchers are particularly sensitive to cues ("information scent") that suggest that their next step will lead them closer to the information they are seeking, without wasting their time (Pirolli & Card 1999). Eye-tracking studies demonstrate where attention rests as a viewer scans a webpage. On results pages, the eye is generally drawn to a "golden triangle" at the upper left corner, paying the most attention to the first result on the page, and gradually less to each of the subsequent results (Granka, Joachims, & Gay 2004). This miserly defense of attention seems to be a learned behavior, and more common among more experienced searchers (Aula, Päivi, & Räihä 2005).

Few of these approaches move beyond the screen to effectively observe the searcher directly, rather than just documenting her transactions. User-centered design has pushed developers to take into account the physical contexts and intentions of their users and how they behave when they interact with the computer. Sophisticated use of log data can allow researchers to infer some of the context for searching (e.g., Adar et al. 2007) and to detect broad patterns (Beitzel et al. 2004). Unlike log data, which can be collected relatively easily and automatically, and surveys, which often rely on accurate self-reflection, direct observation of users engaged in search activities is expensive, time-consuming, and can ultimately be very valuable. Eszter Hargittai (2002b) and others have led recent efforts to make sense of the process of search from a perspective that goes beyond the interface level, and seeks to understand the motivations and social imperatives that shape the experience of search. As she notes, logs fail to provide data about how people react to events in the interfaces – the degree, for example, to which they are satisfied or frustrated by their searches.

The adaptive search engine

In the above study of adolescent searchers, when given a question to answer, more than a quarter typed that question into a search engine. From the perspective of more traditional information retrieval systems, such an approach is naïve and ineffective, but that model of information seeking was changing even before the web came along (Belkin, Oddy, & Brooks 1982). Search engines have answered the challenge by creating engines geared specifically to question-asking (Ask.com), and by assuming that search terms are only part of a phrase when specifically constrained. So, for example, Google will interpret the search *How many actors have played James Bond?* as a search for pages that contain each of those words separately, and among the first few results are several that answer that question. Perhaps, then, the issue is not more sophisticated searchers, but more sophisticated search engines.

The evidence suggests that in some ways users continue to want the same things from search engines they have always wanted: answers. On the other hand, their interactions with search engines evolve even as the search engines change. We can turn to the most basic source of data, the queries themselves, for some evidence of this. A group of researchers compared queries on the Excite search engine in 1997, 1999, and 2001 (Spink et al. 2002). There was a shift during the period from seeking pornography to finding information about commerce, shopping, and work. Contrary to what you might expect, it did not seem that users became more adept at using the Excite search engine during this four-year period. The style of people's queries changed very little over the period, and their willingness to dig beyond the first page of results was reduced. The authors conclude that search engines need to improve, in order to "assist users with query construction and modifica-tion, spelling, and analytical problems that limit their ability or willingness to persist in finding the information they need."

Search engines continue to slowly evolve to meet the needs of the searchers. One of the greatest challenges to search, and something that is fairly obvious when studying search logs, is that people incorrectly spell keywords related to their search. One way to help users find what they are looking for was to help them use keywords that are correctly spelled, and there-fore more likely to appear in the target documents. Simple spell check against static word lists represented a good first step, but spelling errors were even more common for items like the proper names of people and places.[3] Google has har-nessed our collective ability to spell, and, by grouping near-misses, can suggest a more popular spelling.

This approach extends to other areas. Over time, and billions of queries, it may be possible to notice certain consis-tencies among query terms. Someone searching for "John," "Paul," and "George," the engine could suggest, may also want to include "Ringo." By tracking which links are clicked, search engines can provide something akin to a voting system. If the top result for a search for "Mars" is consistently avoided, it is likely that, despite whatever algorithm led to it being placed at the top of the results list, it is not much use to searchers, as a rule.

A significant portion of search engine research now focuses on understanding the web, rather than the user. Rather than merely creating an index that indicates what terms appear on various pages, or what the link structure might suggest about the importance of a page, these efforts try to discover what con-cepts are important on a page, and how this concept or topic might relate to other pages (e.g., Dittenbach, Berger, & Merkl 2006). The Text REtrieval Conferences (TREC) have turned an eager eye toward the web in recent years, and support efforts to provide for understanding of web content in order to aid searching.

These kinds of redesign of the search engine's processes and interface are generally a long-cycle response to user behavior. Even the development of vertical search engines to meet the needs of a perceived subgroup represents this sort of slow evolution. There is also the more immediate response to individuals' particular contexts for a search, or their searching history. Broadly, we can refer to these as "personalization": an ongoing response to users that focuses on their individual needs.

In particular, the rapid increase of mobile users of search engines allows for the user interface to respond "on the fly." Because mobile search behavior tends to be different from search behavior at the desktop, and because it appears that mobile searching may come to be the most common context for the use of search engines, understanding how it differs from desktop search and how to react to those differences is important (Church et al. 2007). At a very basic level, many search engines make use of alternative style sheets to present themselves differently on a small mobile device from how they might be presented on a larger display, but they are now extending this to include information that is more likely to be geospatially relevant, and providing results pages that are more easily read on a mobile device. A recent experimental design provided mobile searchers with access to other query terms that had been used in the same physical location by other users (Jones et al. 2007). These uses of contextual cues provide ways of reducing the complexity of search.

Search engine personalization allows the engine to be reconfigured on the fly. In some cases, the searcher can customize the engine by directly altering how it appears and functions. On the Aftervote metasearch engine, for example, users can indicate whether they want beginner, intermediate, or advanced interfaces, as well as how to weight the results from various search engines, whether to blacklist certain sites, and how results are presented. Personalization can also occur without any sort of direct input from searchers (Pitkow et al. 2002).

Google News, for example, monitors which stories people select and provides similar stories on its "recommended" portion of the page. Search personalization represents one of the most active areas of research, but, as with search generally, by privileging certain sources over others there is the danger that a searcher can become trapped by her own search history.

The adaptive society

Google's corporate history notes that when founders Larry Page and Sergey Brin were initially looking for a buyer for the technology that would become Google, one portal CEO told them, "Our users don't really care about search" (Google 2007). In retrospect, such a comment appears staggeringly myopic, but it was probably not inaccurate. Users did not care about search until they learned what it was and came to depend on it. The changes that have come about with the rise of the search engine have been wider than search skills or search engine prowess. We are essentially information-driven creatures, and when the primary way in which we navigate our informational world changes, it is fair to assume that those changes will pervade other parts of our culture.

The availability of a search engine and easily searched data makes traditional forms of information organization seem tedious and dated. The vertical file that brought the industrial revolution into the office is slowly giving way to the power of search. Using files, like using maps and newspaper indexes, is not a natural skill, and, as our search engine expertise increases, we may lose some of our familiarity with those earlier technologies of findability. Unfortunately, these earlier ways of knowing may have appealed to different kinds of knowledge.

An article in the *San Francisco Chronicle* described the operations of that city's new citywide information line that could be reached by residents and visitors dialing 311 within the city limits (Colin 2007). Initially intended as a way to have a single phone number for all city services, many of the calls were not so easy to connect to a city department. The article explains the calls as modern human nature molded by search engines: "Anonymity. Technology. Excessive information gathering. The elements of 311 are very much those of the Internet age (do people still say that?), and in ways the service resembles a kind of Google hotline just for San Francisco. As with Google, it seems the service can give rise to the questions, rather than vice versa." There can be little doubt that search engines have made the web more useful and provide a valuable service, but to return to the question asked by Plato in the *Phaedrus*, what have we lost with these changes?

There are many answers to that question. Martin Nussbaum, a partner in a large New York law firm, recently spoke about his experience with information technology in legal research. He said he was enthusiastic about the way in which technology makes it possible to quickly and easily search for relevant material when preparing for a case. Although not necessarily happy about how information technology had affected other elements of being an attorney, he saw this change as clearly positive. But, upon reflecting on his early days as a new attorney, in the physical law library of his firm, he remembered that there was once more of an opportunity for serendipity, discovery, and learning that may not be as likely with the new searchable sources.

Serendipity was inherent to the initial metaphor for traversing the web: surfing. The metaphor suggested that while you may be moving through the information, there was room to turn around, or take detours, and that the topography of the information encouraged these actions. In the case of Wikipedia, a new term has emerged for the process of wandering from entry to entry: wikipedestrian. There is a particular knowledge that is obtained only through exploration that is, even when goal-oriented, open to peripatetic friction. There is room for the web *flâneur*, who has gained an understanding of an area not through the accumulation of facts, but by making a large number of wrong turns.

Serendipity is enjoyable, but it is also important to innova-tion, Robert Merton argues in his fascinating history of the con-cept, entitled *The travels and adventures of serendipity* (Merton & Barber 2003). Although searching for materials may seem to be antithetical to serendipity, which has more affinity with brows-ing than with searching, the above description of "berrypicking" suggests it is a part of the experienced searcher's retinue of skills. Consider someone who goes to a search engine hoping to find a particular product; unless it is the first "hit" on the search engine, and the searcher visits only that site, they are likely to spend some time browsing through the results (Rowley 2002). In other words, searching retains a significant amount of brows-ing. Indeed, a good system for searching should incorporate what Smith (1964) termed "systematic serendipity."

Another answer is that students – from kindergarten through graduate school – are using recorded knowledge in new ways. Many people see these as diminished ways, and teachers com-plain about cut-and-paste essays hastily assembled out of web-based resources. As with serendipity, this is a two-edged sword. Expert users of search engines are able to assemble a much wider range of resources from their armchair than students might have been able to in the university library a decade ago. The kinds of sources they use are clearly changing, but whether these represent somehow a diminution of students' research capabilities remains an open question. Students rightly ques-tion why they should be responsible for memorizing facts that are frequently discoverable on the web at a moment's notice. On the other hand, the availability of such information quickly and easily may make it more difficult to create the kinds of connec-tions that lead to deeper knowledge and wisdom.

If we assume that all knowledge can be available on the web, and that such knowledge can be effectively indexed, the idea that we are becoming search-engine-minded is not troubling. If, on the other hand, we take it as a given that knowledge is not just a process of accumulating facts, but involves the experi-ence of learning by doing, the idea that answers are always as near as our favorite search engine is problematic. We understand that the educated person possesses a mastery of latent knowledge, "similar in kind to the inarticulate knowledge of knowing one's way about a complex topography, but [with] its range enhanced by the aid of verbal and other linguistic pointers, the peculiar manageability of which enables us to keep track of an immense amount of experience and to rest assured of having access, when required, to many of its countless particulars" (Polanyi [1952] 1998, p. 103). Many decry the lack of technical education and of computer literacy, and, as we have seen, a secondary digital divide exists between those who are able to find information online and those who are not, but at the same time we must seek to avoid the totalizing effects that the fact-oriented search engines seem to encourage.

Arno Penzias (1989) links intelligence to the ability to ask "questions which illuminate." In this, he is hardly alone; the idea that real wisdom comes from finding and asking probative questions is a fairly common one (Arlin 1990). Given that, should we not be concerned by a machine that changes our daily experience of asking questions. It is not too strange to think about the ways in which our technical environment affects our everyday interaction. The popular press is rife with examples of how instant messaging is bleeding over into other forms of communication. If we become accustomed to asking questions of search engines in ways that are necessarily different from those we might ask of another human, can there be any doubt that this will change the way in which we think and interact?

The issues surrounding student use of search engines raise another concern: is there a systematic bias on the web? If so, what is the nature of that bias? What effect does this have on our collected knowledge and ability to govern ourselves? The next chapter approaches this particular question of changes, dangers, and opportunities arising from the very nature of the web and the role of search engines in it.

CHAPTER THREE

Attention

The telephone may have been invented by Alexander Graham Bell, along with a host of contemporary competitors, but what we think of as the telephone today owes a great deal to a pioneer who may be less familiar. Bell found a way of carrying voice over a telegraph line. When it was first put into use, lines would be run directly between locations that needed to share information, generally between the factory and office. Eventually, networks were created. Some of these were actually broadcast networks: designed to distribute news and entertainment to many telephones at once (Marvin 1988). The more popular private, point-to-point use required human operators to connect people who wanted to talk to one another. At the turn of the nineteenth century, Almon Strowger was one of two undertakers in Kansas City, Missouri, and the other undertaker's wife worked as a telephone operator. Not surprisingly, his rival's mortuary received most of the calls from the recently bereaved in search of funeral services. Frustrated, he devised the Strowger switch, and slowly telephone systems did away with operators in favor of direct dial capabilities (Brenner 1996). This pattern is familiar: just as the telephone switch attempted to automate the role of the operator, search engines stepped in to take the place of those who categorized the web by hand.

No doubt, however, a modern Strowger would be equally frustrated with today's search engine. A search on Live.com for morticians in Kansas City yields 24,310 hits. It seems unlikely that the bereaved would bother with more than the first handful of these. With billions and billions of webpages, and millions more being created daily, there is no way to present them all equally. Some are better, more useful, more interesting pages than others, and we need help finding those pages. The successful search engine does this: it is a technology as much of ignoring as it is of presenting. Who gets to affect that process of selection and who benefits from that process remain open questions.

Gaining attention has always been important to commerce, as well as to the advance of ideas. The ways in which attention is concentrated and distributed are changing rapidly, and the search engine is today's equivalent of the post office or telephone exchange. In an attention economy, those hoping to capture the desires and interest of consumers have struggled with this new structure, and continue to try to understand how to profit from the ways search reconfigures our information and the greater communication landscape.

The web is not flat

The nineteenth and twentieth centuries saw a revolution in mass media, tied to what is often called "the second industrial revolution." The mechanized production of consumer goods extended to publishing, and the improvement of steam-driven presses and new kinds of paper and ink allowed for the creation of the penny press. Perhaps equally importantly, mass production of consumer goods necessitated a mass market, and mass advertising, something the penny press both allowed and necessitated (Schudson 1978). By the time electric media provided broadcast capability, the idea of a one-to-many model of communication had already become commonplace, and the power of the mass media to affect the economy well known. The advertising-supported model of media developed in the penny press was often adopted by the broadcast media.

The penny press represented a major shift in control over the way in which information was distributed. No longer would the political elite have a stranglehold on public discourse; newspapers established a public sphere, a watch-dog, a Fourth Estate. But in creating this counterweight, they established their own hold on discourse. Schudson notes James Fenimore Cooper's 1835 assessment of the new distribution of power: "If newspapers are useful in overthrowing tyrants, it is only to establish a tyranny of their own. The press tyrannizes over publick men, letters, the arts, the stage, and even over private life" (Cooper 2004, p. 118).

The internet and the web likewise have been disruptive to the way attention is aggregated and distributed, and so it is worth asking whether there is a similar "tyranny of the web." To many, the very idea seems strange. After all, the distributed, networked nature of the web suggests a radical lack of hierarchy, an idea expressed emphatically in John Perry Barlow's "Declaration of the independence of cyberspace" in 1996. That document declared the culture of the internet as independent from government intervention, because cyberspace was a world in which everyone could have an equal say: "We are creating a world that all may enter without privilege or prejudice accorded by race, economic power, military force, or station of birth. We are creating a world where anyone, anywhere may express his or her beliefs, no matter how singular, without fear of being coerced into silence or conformity." In overturning the Communications Decency Act, which outlawed indecent speech on the internet, the US Supreme Court echoed an earlier court's opinion that "the content on the Internet is as diverse as human thought" (*Reno* v. *ACLU*, 1997), and as such should not be restricted in the way broadcast media is. One of the justifications for regulating broadcast media is that, since only a limited number of voices may be heard, they naturally favor certain viewpoints over others. Implicit in the Supreme Court's argument is that the web gives a voice to everyone.

The assumption that computer networks are more democratic, and necessarily provide a greater voice to everyone, is probably misguided (Elmer 2006). As Ithiel de Sola Pool (1983) argued persuasively, while the distributed nature of computer networking may make it less inherently likely to become a medium controlled by a relatively small number of interests, equality can only occur if public policy is designed to maintain the balance of the medium. Any careful examination of the web today shows that it is anything but a level, unvariegated network. Some sites get more attention than others, and this is hardly by accident. Search engines both contribute to the selection of the more prominent sites, and in turn are more influenced by them.

One of the reasons that people assume that the internet is a technology that supports a diversity of content is that publishing material on the web is relatively effortless. Unlike broadcast television or radio – or even printing – it is easy for many people to publish to a large, potentially global, audience. In the early days of the web, it might have required learning a bit of HTML, and becoming familiar with FTP and web server technologies, but today the skills necessary to start a blog or upload pictures or video to a cost-free sharing site are almost trivial. One survey showed that 44 percent of adult internet users in the United States have made their own content for the web (Lenhart, Horrigan, & Fallows 2004). But it is entirely likely that any given exposition on the web will be lost in the flood of similar efforts. Of the millions of blogs in the blogosphere and videos on YouTube, most get viewed by only one or two people, while a small number get millions of hits – far from equal access to the greater web audience.

Even if we were to assume that attention to pages on the web was evenly distributed, it is hard to imagine that the hyperlinked structure of the web could be equally "flat." Assuming that every page on the web had eight hyperlinks leaving it, and that the targets of these links were picked at random from all the possible sites on the web, the structure would be entirely unnavigable. Unlike the telephone, the web is very malleable, able to take on the characteristics not just of a point-to-point network or of a broadcast network, but a multitude of shapes between the two (Agre 1998). Links are a valuable way of establishing meaning across pages, and they tend to make the web "chunky." Once cliques or clusters of websites are established, they tend to reinforce themselves. A reader might find site A by following a link from site B, and decide to link to both of them. This sort of linking can tend toward a process of Balkanization (Van Alstyne & Brynjolfsson 1996), which is particularly troubling when it comes to political discourse (Hindman, Tsioutsiouliklis, & Johnson 2003), but it is also a central feature of collective sense-making. Over the last several years, a number of researchers have written about the hyperlinked structure of the web and how it changes over time. It appears that the natural tendency of the web (and of many similar networks) is to link very heavily to a small number of sites: the web picks winners.

Or, to be more accurate, the collective nature of our browsing picks winners. As users forage for information, they tend to follow paths that are, in the aggregate, predictable (Huberman et al. 1998). Huberman (2001) notes that not only are these patterns for surfing the web regular, the resulting structure of the web itself exhibits a number of regularities, particularly in its distribution of features. The normal distribution of features found everywhere – the bell-shaped curve we are familiar with – is also found in places on the web, but, for a number of features, the web demonstrates a "power law" distribution. George Kingsley Zipf (1949) described a similar sort of power law distribution (Zipf's Law[1]) among words in the English language, showing that the most frequently used English word ("the") appears about twice as often as the second most frequently used word ("of"), which appears about twice as often as the third-ranked word, and so on. This distribution – frequency inversely proportionate to rank – has shown up in a number of places, from the size and frequency of earthquakes to city populations.

The number of "backlinks," hyperlinks leading to a given page on the web, provides an example of such a distribution. If the number of backlinks were distributed normally, we would expect for there to be a large number of sites that had an average number of backlinks, and a relatively small number of sites that had very many or very few backlinks. For example, if the average page on the web has 2.1 backlinks (Pandurangan, Raghavan, & Upfal 2002), we might expect that a very large number of pages have about 2 backlinks, and a somewhat smaller number have 1 or 3 backlinks. In practice, a very large number of pages have no backlinks at all, a much smaller number garner only a single backlink, and a smaller number still have 2 backlinks. The average is as high as 2.1 because of the handful of pages that attract many millions of backlinks each. Were human height distributed in a similar fashion, with an average height of, say, 2.1 meters, we would find most of the globe's population stood well under a meter tall, except for a handful of giants who looked down at us from thousands of kilometers in the sky.

Huberman notes that this distribution is "scale-free"; that is, the general nature of the distribution looks the same whether you are examining the entire World Wide Web, or just a small subset of pages, though there may be some web communities in which the effect is not as pronounced (Pennock et al. 2002). I have been blogging for several years, and each blog entry ends up on its own page, often called a "permalink" among bloggers. I examined the most recent 1,500 of my posts, to see how many backlinks each one received. Figure 3.1 shows a ranked distribution of incoming links, not including the first-ranked posting. As of the middle of 2007, the vast majority (1,372) of these 1,500 pages did not have any incoming links at all. Despite this, the average number of backlinks is 0.9, driven upward by the top-ranked posts. Incidentally, as figure 3.2 shows, the number of comments on each of these entries follows a similar distribution, with a very large number of posts (882) receiving either a single comment or none at all. In order to make these figures more legible, I have omitted the most popular post, entitled "How to cheat good," which was the target of 435 backlinks by August of 2007, and had collected 264 comments.[2]

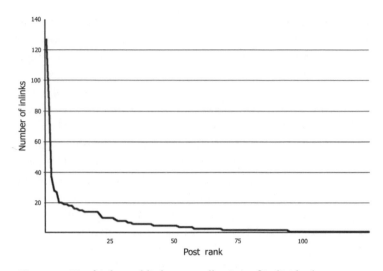

Figure 3.1 Total inbound links to a collection of individual posts on
        alex.halavais.net, ranked by popularity (first-ranked post
        omitted)

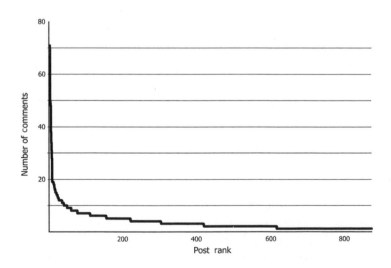

Figure 3.2 Total comments to a collection of individual posts on
        alex.halavais.net, ranked by popularity (first-ranked post
        omitted)

One explanation of such a distribution assumes that there were a few pages at the beginning of the web, in the early 1990s, and each year these sites have grown by a certain percentage. Since the number of pages that were created has increased each year, we would assume that these older sites would have accumulated more hyperlinks over time. Such an explanation is as unlikely on the web as it is among humans. We do not grow more popular with every year that passes; indeed, youth often garners more attention than age. There are pages that are established and quickly become successes, linked to from around the web. While it cannot explain the initial rise in popularity, many of these sites gain new backlinks because they have already received a large number of backlinks. Because of the structure of the web, and the normal browsing patterns (and, as we shall see, the construction of most search engines), highly linked pages are likely to attract ever more links, a characteristic Huberman refers to as "preferential attachment." Such preferential attachment is the mechanism responsible for how hits happen offline, as well, but the explicit nature of linking online, and the rapidity with which novelty can be endorsed, make the web a hot-house environment for "hits" (Farrell 1998).

Take, for example, my most popular recent posting. The earliest comments and links came from friends and others who might regularly browse my blog. Some of those people linked to the site in their own blogs, including law professor Michael Froomkin, on his blog, Discourse.net. From there, the site was eventually linked to from Bruce Schneier's popular Schneier on Security, and, having reached a wider audience, a link was posted to it from Boing Boing, a very popular site with millions of readers. Naturally, many people saw it on Boing Boing and linked to it as well, from their blogs and gradually from other websites. After several months, I received emails telling me that the page had been cited in a European newspaper, and that a printed version of the posting had been distributed to a university's faculty.

It is impossible for me or anyone else to guess why this particular posting became especially popular, but every page on the web that becomes popular relies at least in part on its initial popularity for this to happen. The exact mechanism is unclear, but after some level of success, it appears that popularity in networked environments becomes "catching" (or "glomming"; Balkin 2004). The language of epidemiology is intentional. Just as social networks transmit diseases, they can also transmit ideas, and the structures that support that distribution seem to be in many ways homologous.

Does this mean that this power law distribution of the web is an unavoidable social fact? The distribution certainly seems prevalent, not just in terms of popularity on the web, but in a host of distributions that are formed under similar conditions. More exactly, the power law distribution appears to encourage its own reproduction, by providing an easy and conventional path to the most interesting material. And when individuals decide to follow this path, they further reinforce this lopsided distribution. Individuals choose their destination based on popularity, a fully intentional choice, but this results in the winner-take-all distribution, an outcome none of the contributors desired to reinforce; it is, to borrow a phrase from Giddens, "everyone's doing and no one's" (1984, p. 10). This sort of distribution existed before search engines began mining linkage data, but has been further reinforced and accelerated by a system that benefits from its reproduction.

In the end, the question is probably not whether the web and the engines that search it constitute an open, even, playing field, or even, as Cooper had it with newspapers, "whether a community derives most good or evil, from the institution" (Cooper 2004, p. 113). Both questions are fairly settled: some information on the web is more visible than other information. We may leave to others whether or not the web is, in sum, a good thing; the question has little practical merit as we can hardly expect the web to quietly disappear any time soon. What we may profitably investigate is how attention is guided differently on the web from how it has been in earlier information environments, and who benefits from this.

PageRank

By the end of the 1990s search engines were being taken seriously by people who produced content for the web. This was particularly true of one of the most profitable segments of the early web: pornography. Like many advertising-driven industries, "free" pornography sites were often advertising-supported, and in order to be successful they needed to attract as many viewers as possible. It did not really matter whether or not the viewer was actually looking for pornography – by attracting them to the webpages, the site would probably be paid by the advertiser for the "hit," or might be able to entice the visitor into making a purchase. The idea of the hawker standing on the street trying to entice people into a store is hardly a new one. Search engines made the process a bit more difficult for those hawkers. In fact, for many search engines, securing their own advertising profits required them to effectively silence the pornographers' hawkers.

Search engines were trying to avoid sending people to pornography sites, at least unless the searcher wanted that, which some significant proportion did. What they especially wanted to avoid was having a school-aged child search for information on horses for her school report and be sent – thanks to aggressive hawking by pornography producers – to an explicit site, especially since in the 1990s there was a significant amount of panic (particularly in the United States) about the immoral nature of the newly popular networks. Most advertisers have a vested interest in getting people to come to their site, and are willing to do whatever they can in order to encourage this. Google became the most popular search engine, a title it retains today, by recognizing that links could make it possible to understand how the webpage was regarded by other authors. They were not the first to look to the hyperlinked structure of the web to improve their search results, but they managed to do so more effectively than other search engines had. Along with good coverage of the web, a simple user interface, and other design considerations, this attention to hyperlink structure served them well.

Google and others recognized that hyperlinks were more than just connections, they could be considered votes. When one page linked to another page, it was indicating that the content there was worth reading, worth discovering. After all, this is most likely how web surfers and the search engine's crawlers encountered the page: by following links on the web that led there. If a single hyperlink constituted an endorsement, a large number of links must suggest that a page was particularly interesting or worthy of attention. This logic, probably reflecting the logic of the day-to-day web user, was amplified by the search engine. Given the need to sort through thousands of hits on most searches, looking at the links proved to be helpful.

Take, for example, a search for "staph infections." At the time of writing, Google reports nearly 1.3 million pages include those words, and suggests some terms that would help to refine that search (a feature of their health-related index). The top result, the one that the most people will try, is from Columbia University's advice site Go Ask Alice; the hundredth result is a page with information about a pain-relieving gel that can be used for staph infections; and the last page listed (Google only provides the first several hundred hits) is a blog posting. Gathering link data from search engines is not particularly reliable (Thelwall n.d.), but AltaVista reports that these three sites receive 143, 31, and 3 inbound hyperlinks, respectively.[3] People search for things for very different reasons, but the Columbia site represents a concise, authoritative, and general overview of the condition. The last result is a blog entry by someone who is writing about her husband's recent infection, and while it certainly may be of interest to someone who is faced with similar circumstances, it does not represent the sort of broad information most people searching for the topic are probably looking for.

Evaluating the number of backlinks alone can provide a useful indicator, but, on the web, not all links are equal. The earlier example of my blog is instructive: the most popular posts have been linked to from Boing Boing. Because Boing Boing has a large audience, those links are, in some way, "weightier" than a link from a less widely read site. I may value the link from a friend more highly, but, because of the traffic commanded by Boing Boing, it is safe to assume that a large number of people will become interested in a link from that site. Treating all links as an equal vote is a bit like treating all roads the same when some are driveways and others are multi-lane highways.

Sergei Brin and Larry Page turned to citation analysis for a guide on how to avoid the "junk" on the web and provide higher precision in the search results of the search engine they designed, Google. They assigned a PageRank to each page in the search engine's index, calculated by looking at the PageRanks of the sites pointing to it as well as the number of links from each of those pages to alternatives sites, and an adjustable "damping factor" that adds something like a transaction cost to the reputational boost given by each page (Page et al. 1998). Intuitively, PageRank represents the likelihood that a surfer who is engaging in information foraging will end up at a given page. Hyperlinks might be thought of, in this model, as a series of tubes, conveying what is sometimes called "Googlejuice." Those pages that collect more Googlejuice are also able to pass it along to other webpages.

PageRank tends to reinforce the mechanism of preferential attachment. Preferential attachment occurs in large part because those authors who create hyperlinks are assumed to locate the authoritative pages by surfing the web. Much of the browsing and searching process now occurs within search engines, but since PageRank posits a "model surfer" within the PageRank algorithm, it tends to recreate and enforce the process of preferential attachment. In order for a website to make it onto the first page of results on Google, it first has to have a large number of links to it. However, without being on the first page of results, few website authors will know that it exists and be able to link to it. Every author is then faced with the question of how to draw enough attention to their pages to allow them to be seen by large audiences. PageRank and related esteem-enhancing search algorithms clearly increase the current imbalance, calcifying existing networks of popularity (J. Cho & Roy 2004).

A. J. Liebling famously quipped that "freedom of the press is limited to those who own one." He was wrong; owning the press is not enough, you must have people read what you have published. Perfect distribution of information is limited by our collective attention span. This is a problem for anyone who wants to persuade, from commercial producers to political activists.

An attention economy

In September of 2006, an online diamond retailer called Skyfacet.com was selling jewelry worth about $3 million each year, when a change in Google's ranking algorithms knocked the site off of the first few pages of results for popular queries about jewelry. The result: sales dropped by 17 percent in three months (Greenberg 2007). This is not at all a unique occurrence: Answers.com saw its traffic drop 28 percent after such an algorithm change, with direct financial consequences (Answers.com 2007). In real life, bricks-and-mortar retail sales, much of a shop's success is determined by "location, location, location." It is not all that different in the online world. In both cases, where you are determines how often you get seen and by whom, and for commercial sites, that attention determines how many sales you are able to make.

The structure of the web and the demand for search engines are both, in large part, determined by a single factor: our limited span of attention. Or to put it another way, people wish to gain something with as little effort expended as possible. In information science, this is often referred to as the "principle of least effort," part of the title of a 1949 book by George Zipf. There is a relationship here between limits on individuals' capability to attend to something and the evolution of social networks. When faced with a search task, and most cognitive tasks are search tasks to some extent, people will generally "satisfice": attempt to use only the minimum amount of time and effort necessary to accomplish their information search to some satisfactory level (Simon 1956). It is tempting to see this lack of will to seek out optimal matches to their information-seeking goals as laziness or velleity, but it is a natural conservative function of human cognition. As George Miller (1956) maintained in his famous article on the "magic number seven," "The span of absolute judgment and the span of immediate memory impose severe limitations on the amount of information that we are able to receive, process, and remember." This limited processing, however, leads to efficient foraging, both in the original sense (Carmel & Ben-Haim 2005), and in the case of seeking information.

The web increases the amount of information available to a person, but it does not increase the capacity for consuming that information. We are even less likely to read through the entire web than we would be to read through an entire library. The most important change the web brings us is not this increase of information of various sorts, from detailed astronomical observations to videos of grotesque skateboarding accidents, nor is it the fact that this information is accessible to a much more dispersed audience than ever before. The real change on the web is in the technologies of attention, the ways in which individuals come to attend to particular content.

Over a period of two centuries, the greatest challenge for mass media has been to improve distribution of a single message. As distribution became nearly ubiquitous, particularly with networked broadcasts of radio and television, attention could be concentrated to a greater degree than ever before. The term "broadcast" is perhaps misleading: the television program or major newspaper is instead a mechanism for collecting attention. The media famously tell us not what to think, but what to think about (Cohen 1963). They set the public agenda, and have been instrumental in drawing together common views of what is important. The most significant change brought about by the web is in how attention is distributed. Even if the web is far from flat, it provides a much larger number of options than does the television remote or newspaper stand. Advertisers, who rely on "eyeballs" for their messages, are on the front lines of these changes, and are looking for new ways to aggregate attention.

Herbert Simon, who introduced the idea that information-seekers tend to satisfice rather than optimize, also foresaw the emergence of an attention economy as new sources of information were made available. In 1971, he wrote that "a wealth of information creates a poverty of attention and a need to allocate that attention efficiently among the overabundance of information sources that might consume it" (Simon 1971, pp. 40–1). Simon was before his time. The recent explosion of networked media, and particularly the amateur media production that has occurred during the 2000s, means that attention is now a scarcer commodity than it has ever been before, and there is a renewed interest in the idea of an attention economy.

When we think of attention as something with tradable worth, it provides a new perspective on how media are consumed – or rather on how media audiences are consumed. The web surfer is not just a target of various persuasive messages, but rather someone who is providing attention in return for information. That attention is a valuable commodity. You are presently reading a book, and giving me your attention in the process. I can use that attention myself, or perhaps include advertising in the margins, selling your attention to eager buyers. The attention economy is attractive to advertisers and advertiser-supported media because it provides a model that allows for wealth and power to be measured not in terms of traditional currency, but in the ability to consistently attract attention (Goldhaber 1997). In an attention economy, the search engine is the ultimate aggregator of such wealth, and advertisers are the clearest source of revenue.

Spam, counter-spam

Ranking is inherent to the functioning of most (though not all) search engines, and, anywhere there is a ranking, there are those who wish to move upward. From early on, search engine designers and web producers have played a game of cat-and-mouse. Search engines have sought out results that made them competitive, while web producers found ways of doing the same. In the latter case, this has yielded a new industry: search engine optimization (SEO). SEO practitioners range from the small-audience blogger, hoping to rise a bit in the Technorati rankings by "link slutting" (J. Walker 2005), to the "enhancement drugs" flogger, creating link farms to enhance his position on Google. Really, anyone who wants their message heard by a large audience must find a way onto the results pages of various search engines. If there is an emerging attention economy, the search engine is its trading floor.

When the first spam message appeared, it was fairly easy to identify. Until lifted by the National Science Foundation in 1994, there was an unofficial ban on commercial activity on the internet, enforced by cultural pressures. When the Digital Equipment Corporation sent a broadcast email advertising the release of one of their new systems in 1978, it met a sharp rebuke from the recipients. The problem was not necessarily that the email had been sent to a large number of people, but that it contained a commercial message. Soon after the loosening of such restrictions, thousands of Usenet newsgroups received what would become a milestone in spam, an advertisement for immigration legal services from a pair of attorneys in Arizona. Not all spam was commercial in nature (some of the earliest spam consisted of chain letters, or accidentally duplicated messages), and as the 1990s wore on, not all commercial messages were spam. But all spam had one common attribute: it was forced on your attention unbidden (Specter 2007).

The idea, then, that spam could exist on the web is a bit confusing. Webpages do not arrive without being called up. At best, we might think of "clutter," advertisements on a page that are irritating or distract our attention (C.-H. Cho & Cheon 2004). Search engines, however, can become the unwitting host of spam, or what is sometimes called "spamdexing." The initial form of spamdexing involved inserting keywords into a page that were not directly related to the content. These could be inserted in a number of ways. Early search engines were likely to draw from the "keywords" metatag, trusting that the author was best able to determine the content of the page, but these quickly came to be ignored because they were so easily used to deceive. Content creators, however, could use other methods, like large amounts of text made invisible to everyone but the search engine (by making it the same color as the background, for example). They might also "stuff" keywords, by repeating them in a non-visible way over and over again. These keywords might include the names of competitors, or completely unrelated terms that are nonetheless popular at the time (e.g. "Monica Lewinski"). These techniques are generally invisible to the user, but prey on the indexing process of the search engine to subvert its function (Nathanson 1998). Other approaches include a bait and switch that allows the search engine to index a legitimate page, but whisks the user off to an unrelated page if they visit. Sites can also be "cloaked," providing one page to visitors identified as crawlers, and a completely different page to human visitors (Chellapilla & Chickering 2006).

While redirection and keyword-based approaches to tricking their way to the top of results pages are still widely used by spamdexers, many search engines do a good job of uncovering the most obvious examples, and rely more heavily on examining a given page within the larger context of the web. As already noted, Google shifted the way that search engines determine the focus of a site, and no longer fully trust the creator of the page to tell the search engine what can be found there. PageRank provides a way for the web community to tacitly vote on the quality of a page, and Google also extracts keyword information from the text of those links (the "anchor text"), so that the pages pointing to a given page take on a greater role in describing it. Unfortunately, these approaches can also be compromised through link spam, and Googlebombing.

In the earlier discussion of PageRank, we encountered three examples of results for a search for "staph infection." The hundredth result in this search was a site providing information from a manufacturer about a pain-relieving treatment, a site that received hyperlinks from 31 other pages. Browsing through these pages makes clear that most of them have little content at all, and consist only of links to other pages and advertising. When spamdexers recognized that links mattered, they began looking for ways to increase their backlinks. One way of doing this is to establish a large number of pages, called a "link farm," to link to your target page. These supporting pages probably do not provide a great deal of Googlejuice because they remain relatively unlinked themselves, but in the process of trading out links, some amount of support is created.

Spamdexers are also able to exploit the fact that they can make links on some websites, and particularly on blogs and wikis (Davison, Najork, & Converse 2006). Large blogging platforms like Blogger and Livejournal, because they provide free hosting and an easy way to set up a website, have long been the target of spamdexers who used robots to automatically create "splogs" (spam blogs, or blogs set up as link farms). Blogs tend to be interlinked more than other parts of the web, and they have other attributes that seem attractive to several search engine algorithms: they are frequently updated and change their outbound links, for example. During the early 2000s, so many searches would result in blogs among the top results it aggravated those who saw blogs as undesirable search results (Orlowski 2003). These blogs also represented a wonderful target of opportunity for spamdexers. A link from a well-linked blog or wiki boosts the PageRank, and links from thousands of such sites can be very valuable. As the spamdexers began to take advantage of this, bloggers quickly found their comments inundated with spam messages linking back to the unrelated pages of spammers.

Comments on blogs, or any system that permits them, are doubly effective for the spammer. The messages are viewable by any visitor to the site, and are often automatically emailed to the blog author. But they are also an effective form of link spam, creating links from a high-reputation site, and mis-appropriating small slices of credibility, Googlejuice, from the host site. Since some blogs list other sites on the web who have linked to the blog, another approach has spamdexers tricking the blogs into recording reciprocal links. Cognizant of the negative effects these attacks were having, Google was a strong supporter of a tag that could be placed within links to nullify their effect on PageRank. By including the "nofollow" tag in links left by visitors, the thinking went, a major reason for leaving spam comments would be eliminated, and a significant source of noise in Google's search results could be removed. Though the major blogging systems signed on, it certainly has not spelled an end to blog spam.

Since Google and others now make more extensive use of anchor text, the ability to classify material falls to a greater degree on those who link to it. The paradigmatical example of a Googlebomb was the effort to associate the search term "miserable failure" with the biography of George Bush on the White House website. If enough links to that page included the text "miserable failure," Google would assume that this represented an important topic of the page, even though it did not appear on the page itself. Because of the distributed nature of Googlebombs, they have been used most notably for political purposes, but commercial Googlebombs have also been employed, particularly to discredit competition (Glaser 2005).

Many consider the title "search engine optimization" merely a euphemism for search engine spamming. Those who provide SEO services contend that the difference is that their ethical practices preclude the use of deception. Given the desire by both commercial and non-commercial web producers to have their work well represented by the search engines, it would be fair to suggest that everyone engages in some form of search engine optimization. This starts, as many search engines recommend, with good content and a well-organized website.[4] Even basic introductions to web design provide information about "tuning" for search engines (e.g. Freeman & Freeman 2006). Almost all search engines make use of robot exclusion protocols so that authors have a way of indicating to crawlers what should be ignored, and the major search engines also use XML sitemaps to help crawlers discover and crawl all the important material on a website. All of this effort to be well regarded by the search engines is not just sensible, it is considered good design practice.

The line between good information design and spamdexing is very fuzzy, but it seems to have to do with transparency. The dichotomy largely mirrors arguments over advertising in general. Many consider SEO to be an integral part of a web marketing strategy. There are certainly forms of false advertising that are regulated by governments in various ways, but advertising is never merely matching a consumer's needs to a given product. Advertising involves, fundamentally, the creation of needs. Whether such a creation of needs, at least among adults, is an intrusion or not remains an unanswered question. Nonetheless, the ethics of SEO practices seem to differ depending on where you stand.

Being branded as a spammer by the search engines can have serious consequences. As it was previously noted,

Skyfacet.com saw sales drop off precipitously after being knocked from the top set of results on Google. While it is hard to know exactly why such a change occurred, the owner of the retail site blames a search marketing consultant he hired to help his placement. The consultant duplicated the material on the site across many pages, and the changes made to the site seemed to have just the opposite of the intended effect (Greenberg 2007). When Google detects someone trying to "game the system," they react by penalizing the site, and the result was lower visibility for Skyfacet.com.

While Skyfacet's owner blamed his consultant, perhaps with just cause, the other possibility is that someone made him look like he was trying to game Google, when in fact he was not. Unscrupulous businesses may not be able to move themselves up in Google's rankings directly, but by making competitors appear to be spammers, they can bump them out of the running. This practice, called "Google bowling" by some (Pedone 2005), involves sabotaging competitors' sites by making them appear to be engaging in obvious link farming and other practices used by search spammers.

There are millions of content creators all eager to have their work seen by people who want to see it and who will come away from the experience changed. There are millions of people who want nothing more than to be exposed to one of these pages that will help them to learn what they want to know, and better control their own destinies. Between these huge collections of content producers and consumers is a relatively small number of search engines, switchboards of the internet generation, faced with the task of discovering how best to connect the content with the searchers. This is a complex process. Like a librarian, the search engine is a key to a resource that otherwise is far less useful. It adds significant value to the internet, and running a search engine requires significant capital and creative resources. Is there a mechanism that allows for that value to be expressed, and the work rewarded?

Who pays for search?

In a seminal article describing the Google search engine, S. Brin and Page (1998) include an appendix about advertising on search engines. They claim that Google demonstrated its worth by finding, in a search for mobile phones, an academic article on the dangers of driving while speaking on a mobile telephone, and that "a search engine which was taking money for showing cellular phone ads would have difficulty justifying the page that our system returned to its paying advertisers." They went on to suggest that advertising-driven search engines are "inherently biased" toward the advertisers and away from those who are using the search engine to find the most appropriate material. What a difference a decade makes. A posting on Google's "Health Advertising Blog," for example, suggests ways in which advertising through Google could counterbalance criticism of the health industry by Michael Moore's documentary *Sicko* (Turner 2007). A number of commentators (e.g. Wiggins 2003) have become concerned with the potential for bias in Google's secret ranking algorithm. While Google's major product remains search, in its many varied forms, its main business is advertising.

It is difficult to remember a time when the web was not commercial, and when search was something people expected for free. Brin and Page attribute their thinking on the issue to Bagdikian's influential book *The media monopoly* (1983), which provides evidence that the concentration of the ownership of media leads to imbalances, especially in the news media. With the rapacious acquisitions of today's internet giants, including the Google empire, it is appropriate that they would be interested in Bagdikian's critique. But given the trajectory of the company they founded, which became a publicly traded corporation in 2004, they might have drawn more heavily from the critique leveled by Robert McChesney. McChesney (1996) compared the state of the internet in the 1990s to radio in the 1930s. Radio thrived as an amateur medium in the United

States until its commercialization, with the help of federal regulation that was friendly to industrial giants like RCA. McChesney suggested that in the 1990s the internet seemed to be following the same pattern, and although the nature of the technology might preclude its complete privatization, the dominance of profit-oriented enterprise could make the construction of an effective public sphere impossible. Radio was limited by the broadcast spectrum and only so many people could speak at once. On the internet, anyone can add to the web, but there is a limit on the amount of information that can be effectively attended to by any individual or group. For a while, it seemed as if commercial media producers would monopolize the attention span of web users.

Recent uses of the web to distribute user-created media suggest that commercial producers may not have an unassailable grip on the public's attention. Looking at a list of the most popular websites, it is easy to conclude that the web belongs to commercial interests. With the exception of Wikipedia, we find large internet businesses and especially portals and search engines dominating the top of the charts. But it may be fair to compare the search engine companies to internet service providers. In both cases, although the infrastructure may be privately held, a substantial part of content is not. The email messages on Yahoo mail, the vast majority of the videos on Google's YouTube, and the thousands of blogs on News Corporation's MySpace are created by amateurs. On the other hand, as McChesney argues, without a political culture, even user-created work is unlikely to encourage an active public sphere. It has traditionally been relatively easy to associate mass media with industry and amateur media was (by definition) non-commercial. Search engines have changed this calculus, by automating the identification of niches, and now, with aggregation of the attention paid to those niches, many individuals are able to advertise and sell goods to a global audience.

The argument has been made that Google's main source of income is selling advertising based on content that they do not own, whether or not that content is user-created (Bogatin & Sullivan 2007). People pay attention to ads on sites they trust, and that makes user-generated media a particularly good target for marketers (Fulgoni 2007). Like other search engines, Google now trades the attention of its users for revenue from advertisers who place ads on its site. But Google has gone beyond this, with AdSense, to place advertising across the web, and in the future plans to extend AdSense to advertising within video games, on the radio, and on billboards (Bishop 2007; "Street advertising gets local-stock-savvy" 2007). The relationship between search and advertising may seem strained, but, as Google has learned, there are certain affinities between the two.

When Brin and Page made their remarks, many of the successful search engines were seeking a path to profit. The "dot.com" era was under way, and many were certain that internet-related enterprises would be fabulously profitable, though at times it was not clear just how this would happen. It was apparent that search engines were a central feature of the exploding web, and, especially given that search was a relatively resource-intensive enterprise, search engine companies were eager to locate revenue streams. There were some experiments with subscription-based engines (e.g. Overture, which charged for search engine placements), but these generally gave way to freely available search engines. Advertising made sense from two perspectives. First, search engines were becoming one of the most visited kinds of sites on the web; traffic alone made them attractive. Second, when people went to a search engine, they were often in search of something, and that might make them more prepared to have their interest piqued by a banner ad, or, better yet, an appropriate advertisement right there next to the search results.

Marketers can pay search engines for a number of different kinds of representations. The clearest division between search content and advertising is provided by a banner ad, often one of many randomly rotated on the search engine's pages.

Marketers can also affect the content of the index in some cases, through paid inclusion, or some form of paid inclusion or paid placement. For some time, Yahoo has accepted suggestions of pages to crawl either for free, or for a fee, but with a fee they guarantee more prompt and frequent crawling. As with Google's AdWords, a Pay Per Click (PPC) advertising service for the search engine, ads can be generated as a result of particular keywords. This sort of "paid placement" ad raises concerns, since nearly 80 percent of search engine users have difficulty distinguishing between "organic" results, generated as part of the normal functioning of the search engine, and paid placement advertisements, at times. Almost a third think that too many results are sponsored (Zillmer & Furlong 2006). Except when the search is obviously commercial (e.g. Amazon.com), in order to maintain their reputations as fair arbiters of content, most search engines offer a clear segregation of the paid and organic results (Davenport & Beck 2001, p. 132). At the same time they must also avoid "banner blindness," which will reduce the number of clickthroughs their advertisers receive (Benway & Lane 1998). Paid inclusion and advertising of various sorts now makes up a large part of any SEO consultant's work, and is probably part of the reason the wider term "Search Engine Marketing" is becoming popular.

Google expanded their success with AdWords to allow for web authors to also accept PPC advertising. The ability to easily convert site traffic into revenue using this and similar automated advertising systems has created new kinds of spam problems. The combination of PageRank and AdSense has led to pages that might be considered Google symbionts, or, less charitably, parasites. These are often called "scraper sites," as they gather information from other websites automatically in order to be a highly ranked hit on search engine results pages, and are then covered in ads (often AdSense ads) to return revenue to the person constructing the page.

What may at first appear to be an unholy union between search engines and advertising in fact hints at changes in the way advertisers are thinking about what they do. For more than a decade, expenditures on mass media advertising have indicated that the traditional view of advertising and marketing is dead (Rust & Oliver 1994). Much of this move was toward a broader view of communicating with customers, and understanding what they were looking for in a more personalized way. Both search engine designers and marketers are attempting to meet the practices and evolving needs of a diverse group of users. Online, this means they are focusing more heavily on web analytics and behavioral targeting. By tracking how people search for and find information online, both search engine designers and marketers aim to present information in a more effective way. It should not be surprising that the two are converging, and there are opportunities for changing how people buy and sell things, and what role large corporations play in this process. Many see in these rapid changes an opportunity to counter a different kind of power law, one that favors large producers in the marketplace. As access to advertising is "democratized," they see new opportunities for small-scale producers.

While such a process may open the door to new producers, some argue it only serves to further commodify our social lives online. Ebay may challenge other online sellers, but the (seeming) disintermediation it provides still encourages the continued commodification of online interaction. Likewise, although search engines may potentially provide access to minority opinions and amateur media, and even if those producers do not accept advertising directly, the process of producing and distributing media via advertising-based search engines requires the amateur producer to succumb to technological rationalization inherent to advertising-supported search engines, and to the new forms of "distributed capitalism" (Zuboff & Maxmin 2002) it supports. And the logic of the attention economy dictates how successful our contributions might be, urging us to promote (and produce) novelty over depth or quality – a process Marcuse (1964) referred to as "repressive desublimization."

The scarcity of attention is not artificial. There are real limits to what we can attend to. But the market for attention is a construct that allows for the ideology of the marketplace to be granted access to new areas. This commodification of attention occurs in a largely invisible way. Search engines extract value through the freely given labor of millions of people, and, by reconfiguring it, use it to draw attention to themselves. That attention is then sold to producers who wish to advertise their products. While the internet provides a platform for self-expression, that expression is constrained by the values of the network. This does not remove the potential for the creation of extraordinarily articulate work, demonstrated by parts of Wikipedia, and, as Richard Sennett (2008) suggests, by those who work on the Linux operating system. But it does tend to push such efforts to the margin, and requires that they negotiate within a system of attention and exchange that has become heavily commoditized, and be aware of the tension between truly liberating forms of online communication and maintaining what Stewart Ewen (1976, p. 219) refers to as "an unrelenting vigilance against and rejection of the corporation mode of ameliorization."

The culture of free exchange exemplified by the free software movement and prevalent on the internet from its earliest days continues to win adherents. It suggests that software and other content should be accessible to all, transparent, and unburdened by restrictive licenses. The best bulwark against bias and commodification in search is a wide diversity of search engines (Mowshowitz & Kawaguchi 2002) but, if all of those search engines are supported by advertising, there is the potential that searches will lean inexorably toward commercial enterprises. While they remain at the earliest stages, and still face stubborn challenges, there are several efforts being made to develop free alternatives to the search giants. The prospects for these efforts are addressed in a later chapter; here we need only note that the current search engine industry is dominated by large, profit-seeking corporations, and this affects what we find when we search and how we evaluate it.

The search ecosystem

All of these players, each with their own interests, interact within a larger information ecosystem. Users want to be able to find what they are seeking, no matter whether their goal is unfocused browsing, or a relatively narrow search. Familiarity means that searchers tend to be loyal to a particular general-purpose search engine, and unlikely to switch to another search engine unless there is a significant advantage in doing so. Search engines, whose profits can be measured largely in terms of the attention they draw, must help to deliver on those search goals as quickly and as effortlessly as possible, for as many people as possible. To do that, they must constantly create new ways of keeping content creators in check. Google's ranking algorithm, for example, tracks 200 different factors ("signals") to help determine how an individual page should be ranked (Hansell 2007), and search engine optimizers have identified their own set of signals that seem to affect search engines directly (Fishkin & Pollard 2007). Like most commercial search engines, Google keeps its ranking algorithm secret, to avoid manipulation from content creators. Of course, content creators all seek audiences for their pages, and many are willing to do a great deal to ensure that their page shows up among the first few results on the search engine results pages. After investing in the content, they want to see it delivered, and since attention is a finite good, only those who best understand the way in which search engines operate, or who have a strong network of trusting fans – or just get lucky – will have their content delivered to the right audiences.

As with any complex system, it is difficult to predict how it behaves, and how it might change over time. As long as attention continues to be considered a scarce commodity, we can expect that content creators and search engine developers will continue to engage in a war of increasingly sophisticated means. Some have argued that search engines need to find ways of freeing up content and to minimize the race to visibility (Gori & Witten 2005). As frustrating as the active efforts of spamdexers are, it is worth acknowledging the service they perform by exploiting the weaknesses of search algorithms. It would be nice to believe that mutual trust and assistance between content producers and search engines alone would yield a better and more equitable search environment, but it seems unlikely – now that attention has been so heavily commoditized – that competition among content producers will diminish. That game has never been zero-sum, and there are benefits to the majority when the process is optimized, and when more people are able to find more of what they are looking for with less effort. It is a mistake to assume that network culture does away with the desires manufactured by mass culture. If anything, the ubiquity of advertising represents an increasingly flexible and accelerated extension of mass culture. Although it is difficult to get away from the macro-view, some of the most interesting changes brought about by the internet, and by search technologies in particular, are not at the peak end of attention, but in the long tail of interactions within niche information communities. It may be that developing more equitable search necessarily must occur at the margins.

Advertising quantifies attention in new ways. The internet and the web were developed within a culture of freedom, both in terms of access and speech, and in terms of cost to the user. In that environment, it is tempting to think of the web as flat, and without impediments to participation. When compared to earlier broadcast media, there can be little doubt that the internet provides at least the potential for more equitable access, but a paucity of attention, which drives the need for search technologies, precludes access to everyone by everyone.

CHAPTER FOUR

Knowledge and Democracy

Companies and webmasters are hardly the only groups to recognize that search engines represent a concentration of power. As Karl Deutsch (1966) has argued, communication networks represent a sort of nervous system for the body politic, a means of information and control. The search engine, in this corporeal metaphor, is the spinal cord, and represents a nexus of feedback and control. Given the disruptive nature of a communication network driven by search, rather than by broadcast, many expected a revolutionary change in the structure of knowledge and the nature of politics. Though there are some small fissures that suggest change, search engines as they exist today represent a largely conservative force, increasing the attention paid to those people, institutions, and ideas that have traditionally held sway.

The idealized metaphor for the search engine may be a telescope, allowing us to pick out one star from millions and examine it in more detail. Such an optical metaphor suggests a certain degree of transparency; the search engine does not favor one page over another in this view, but simply selects the few pages among millions that most nearly meet a user's needs. Of course, this is not how search engines work. In the process of ranking results, search engines effectively create winners and losers on the web as a whole. Now that search engines are moving into other realms, this often opaque technology of ranking becomes kingmaker in new venues. The web provides some form of access to what might otherwise be content on the fringe of society, but the most popular search engines tend to subvert this diversity. This chapter engages the tension between the unifying force of the search engine and the diverse content of the web.

The default position of those in the search engine business has often been to claim that the search engine algorithm simply reflects the reality of the web, and that any problems can be overcome by tweaking the technology. For some time, the top-ranked result for a search on Google for Martin Luther King was a site created by a white supremacist group, and, at the time of writing, that site still appears among the first ten search results returned. The views presented by the group are abhorrent to mainstream society, and yet are ranked among those pages created by what many would consider "authorities" in the area, including a biographical site created by *Time* magazine. Then there is the first-ranked site on the page, Wikipedia, a user-editable encyclopedia that has become a controversial source of information on the web. None of these are "naturally" the best first choices, but they are the selections made by the ranking algorithm, the set of processes that help to sort search results to make them more useful to the user.

The issue is two-fold. First, what is it about the technology of search that encourages the division between "winners" and "losers" in the contest for public attention? Second, to what degree do the winners of that game correspond with traditional authorities? Both of these questions are related to the flow of information in society, and the effect this has on discovery and self-governance.

Search engines represent a point of control in those flows of information. Those who use search engines well gain a certain advantage, but we are all used by the search engine to some degree, and come to conform to it. Current search engines, like communication technologies before them, contain both centralizing and diversifying potentials. These potentials affect the stories we tell ourselves as a society, and the way we produce knowledge and wisdom. Designers of search tools, as well as expert users of those tools, are structurally more capable of countering the centralizing and homogenizing effects of the new search technologies, and ethically obligated to act on behalf of those who will otherwise be drawn only to what they find on the top of a search results page.

Search inequality

In examining how adolescents search the web, one research study (Guinee, Eagleton, & Hall 2003) noted their reactions to failed searches. Searchers might try new keywords, or switch search engines, for example. One common reaction was to change the topic, to reframe the question in terms of what was more easily findable via the search engine. The models of search suggest that searchers satisfice: look for sufficiently good answers rather than exhaustively seek the best answer. Because of this, the filters of the search engine may do more than emphasize certain sources over others, they may affect what it is we are looking for in the first place. It is tempting simply to consider this to be poor research skills – or worse, a form of technical illiteracy – but simple answers do not fit this complex problem.

First, we might focus on those doing the searches. A user-centric view places the search engine in the role of grand inquisitor, separating those who are able to search effectively from those who are not. The initial concerns over social inequality on the net had to do with who could gain physical access to the net. This remains important – although there are many more opportunities to get online for many more people, the quality and frequency of the connection varies considerably – but, as we have seen, that physical access to a networked computer is not the same as access to the desired content on the World Wide Web. A divide between skilled and unskilled users of search engines represents a divide between those who can access the breadth of information on the net, and make an informed decision based on multiple sources, and those who are forced to depend on only the most easily found information. There is a relationship between income, race, and particularly education and the ability to find and access information on the web (DiMaggio et al. 2004). If the search engines serve to emphasize and increase already existing gaps in access to knowledge and communication, that represents a significant social challenge.

Differences in social class and education often map themselves onto geography as well. Since the end of the Second World War, the United States has become the central point in a global system of communication. Given the ways in which the United States (and not only the USA) has employed earlier electronic communication technologies to spread an American brand of consumer culture around the world (Schiller 1971), it is easy to mark search engines as a digital comprador, erasing national borders and the role of states in shaping policy. Many of the global media giants are based in the United States, to the extent that they are bound by nation at all. Not only do these transnational corporations distribute content into nearly every corner of the globe, the consumer culture they promote is now found in the alternative, domestically produced content they share the media space with (Sklair 1995, pp. 162–75). In the early days of the internet, there were reasons to be cautiously optimistic about the potential for disrupting the entrenched North–South flow of information and news, and there remain reasons to be hopeful (Hachten 1992, pp. 64–6). Nonetheless, because the United States dominates the search engine market, and because search engines present centralizing tendencies, this particular technology raises special concerns.

The search engine is not a totalizing technology. As noted in the previous chapter, it allows for work at the margins, and the more expert the user, the less influential its bias toward transnational consumer culture. Nonetheless, there is the distinct danger that, as more and more of our collective memories and culture moves online, the existing hegemony will crowd out global cultural diversity (Mattelart 2000). Jean-Noël Jeanneney, who directs the Bibliothèque nationale de France, has seen Google's efforts to digitize major libraries as a challenge for just this reason. He notes, for example, that if Google comes to represent the most easily accessed and readily available source of knowledge on the planet, the ranking of various books in their collection will come to have far-reaching consequences: "I want our children, as they discover the French Revolution, at least to read Victor Hugo's *Quatre-vingt-treize*, or Jean Jaurès's *Histoire Socialiste De La Révolution*, as well as Charles Dickens's very hostile *Tale of Two Cities* or Baroness Orczy's *The Scarlet Pimpernel*, which I enjoyed as a child in the Nelson series (without harm, in my case, because I had antidotes): in the latter we saw ad nauseam those admirable British aristocrats tirelessly pulling their French peers from the bloody clutches of the Terrorists" (2007, p. 42).[1] He ascribes no nefarious motives to Google in particular, but simply notes the natural tendency for an English-language resource to favor a version of the revolution that may not well represent the French perspective. He argues passionately for both book scanning efforts and search engines created and managed in Europe.

A number of search engines have made significant inroads at the national level around the world, but rarely gain a significant user base outside of their home country. The recent rise of the Baidu search engine, appealing to a global Chinese-language audience, is a marked exception in this regard, and although it does not represent a major global challenge to the largest search engines, Baidu continues to gain popularity. Nonetheless, the overall story remains the same: search engines are dominated by American companies, and this in turn suggests an imperial and proprietary relationship to the internet.

With particular exceptions, in which the companies may be asked by the US government to behave in certain ways, we might assume that these companies follow an imperative that makes them uninterested in favoring their home nations. There are, however, national biases: US search engines tend to link to a larger proportion of the total US websites than they do to sites in other countries. As Vaughan and Thelwall (2004) explain, this does not appear to be an issue of linguistic differences, nor a disguised form of xenophobia. Rather, they argue, the difference is likely due to "natural" differences in authority, as determined by the hyperlink structure. In the language of PageRank, US sites simply have more authority: more links leading to them. They note that sites have existed longer in the United States, where much of the early growth of the internet occurred, and that this may give US sites an advantage. Add to this the idea that early winners have a continuing advantage in attracting new links and traffic, and US dominance of search seems a foregone conclusion. Clearly, as argued above, the search engines do not merely reflect this authority, they help to reproduce it.

This assumption that a narrow attention market for sites, with clear winners and losers picked by market forces, is the "natural" configuration for a search engine is the very definition of ideology. [2] Even search engine creators who take a very inclusive view of participatory design are unlikely to be able to encode the cultural understandings of the diversity of global users into their search engine designs. When they judge relevance based on a model user, that model user is likely to resemble the designers themselves. It is difficult to overcome the variety of cultural understandings about how the world is organized. Metaphors of informational spaces and expectations about online social interactions root our interaction with search engines, as they do in interactions with other environments. For Bourdieu (2003), for example, the North African Berber home is a microcosm of the culturally constructed cognitive practices of the occupant, the arrangements of objects betraying an arrangement of thoughts. This difficulty of cultural translation is at the heart of anthropology, and despite the tendency toward a homogeneous "McWorld," particularly online, cultures assign authority in different ways. This accounts in large part for some of the popular nationally and linguistically based search engines, which feel a bit more like home to the user. But the need for broader coverage of a topic often drives users to global search engines, which are overwhelmingly oriented toward the American mainstream and the English language. Architects and designers of physical objects have learned to account for the social and political implications of the diversity of cultures that engage their products. For the designers of information spaces, understanding the cultural substrate that helps people understand how to find things is equally important (Benyon 1998).

As the general-purpose search engines come to encompass ever-increasing portions of our media diet, the potential for such global inequities becomes even greater. A German is likely to draw her news from a major news search engine. But by visiting Google News or Yahoo News, which are both popular options in Germany, she is likely to be exposed to news sources that are English-language-centric and oriented toward the United States (Machill & Beiler 2006). This becomes even more problematic when the precise selection process for the news search, like most search functions, is kept secret (Wiggins 2003).

There are arguments that this is exactly what should happen in a marketplace of ideas. If US news sources manage to attract more attention, that represents the utility of their product; people vote with their mouse-clicks. The problem is that people are not freely able to select a choice from the totality of options. While the system may not be intentionally biased, it acts to aggregate interests toward the most common interest. This structure, based on votes and common interest, may appear to represent a kind of democracy. But because it does not allow for deliberation and discussion at local levels, it makes us into a global mob, easily led by those at the center of attention (Johnson 1997).

As Jeanneney suggests, the "Googlization" of cultural artifacts also diminishes the role of the state in acting as a counter to consumer culture. Policies were put in place in France to protect small booksellers against the giant resellers, and restrictions placed on pricing remaindered books, precisely to preserve a diversity of sellers and content. Governments are charged with protecting the national culture and way of life, and managing the flow of information has traditionally been a part of this. The flow of new sources of information into a country is itself a significant threat to national ideas and ideals. What is worse is that it has the potential to exacerbate the loss of community and traditional institutions, leaving people with even fewer alternatives (Holderness 1998). One of the problems of global transparency is that it reduces the opportunity for nurturing new ideas within a community of likeminded people, without interference from the wider world.

On the other hand, it may be that the real threat is not radical openness, but the formation of cliques in online communities. In its idealized form, the internet provides the powerful opportunity to communicate intersubjective knowledge, allowing people to experience the lives of others very unlike themselves (Warf & Grimes 1997). In particular, user-created media like blogs and videos provide an unprecedented view into the lives of others. In practice, this is a fairly rare occurrence. As Adamic and Glance (2005) found during the 2004 US elections, bloggers are far more likely to link to other likeminded writers than they are to those with differing views. Unfortunately, search engines at present tend to retrench those divides, allowing even further filtering of exposure. Nonetheless, links that reached across issue divides were created, suggesting that with appropriate changes to the technologies, and awareness of how those technologies may be biased, there is a potential for creating more deliberative and diverse online communities.

Knowledge glocalization

An article published in 2001 by DiMaggio et al. asked what effect the web would have on the culture of its users. Would it lead to "bountiful diversity, hypersegmentation, or massification"? Six years later, it appears that it leads in all three of these directions at once. One explanation is that it sits somewhere between centralized and segmented, which Yochai Benkler reveals as a configuration that "if not 'just right,' at least structures a networked public sphere more attractive than the mass-media-dominated public sphere" (2006, p. 239). Rather than a balance, the current structure is a complex combination of a high degree of centralization at the macro-level, with a broad set of diverse divisions at the micro-level. Barber (1996) refers to two forces driving shifts in global politics and business. There is a tendency toward rationalization and standardization of business practices, and a coming together of the globe under the yoke of global capitalism, moving toward "McWorld." At the same time, local culture is re-asserting its uniqueness and desire to remain apart: "Jihad." Barber attributes these changes, in large part, to global communication technologies. The Janus-faced duality he terms "glocalization."

James Carey (1969), writing about another communication technology – the newspaper – notes a similar tendency: centripetal and centrifugal forces unleashed by the penny press. On one side, a geographically dispersed nation like the United States could be bound together when they were reading the same newspaper. At the same time, the rise of newspapers that served distributed groups that historically did not share a public voice – gays, African Americans, and women, for example – allowed for the creation of new communities that were kept connected through this new publishing medium. These two forces in combination led to a newly complex media environment. In the end, many people would probably agree that the unifying forces of mass media have won out. The same is true of search engines: the general-purpose search engines like Google and Yahoo tend to draw global attention to a relatively narrow portion of the web at large. And as we have seen, when it comes to search engines, the rich are likely to get richer. Ideas with current purchase attract more links, and therefore more attention, leading to these ideas existing even as large minorities are being gradually silenced.

The rule of the many even extends to spelling. Until recently, a search for "colours" on google.com led to the suggestion that you may have intended "colors," since more searches occur with this spelling. There is reason in this: if more people search using the Americanized spelling, it may also be that more results are available with that spelling. Of course, given that the search engine already does some synonym checking (a search for the plural "colours," for example, will also include the word "colour"), it seems odd that the engine would not consider the alternate spellings of the word to also be synonymous. And it is worth noting that a search for "colour" at google.co.uk does not lead to a suggestion of the American spelling. It would be wrong to condemn Google entirely for this tendency toward dominant spelling. After all, difficulty with standard spelling can represent a significant obstacle for those who are less educated, or speakers of English as a second language, and spell-checking represents a way to provide these groups with a chance to access material more effectively (Hargittai 2006). But, like other filtering processes, the biases introduced – for perfectly rational reasons – may have pernicious effects on the diversity of information accessible.

Beyond a biased set of results, searchers may be encountering a bias in inquiry. As noted earlier, those who are unable to obtain satisfactory results from a search engine often decide to change their topic and look for something more easily found. More disturbing, and more difficult to measure, is the possibility that search engines encourage us to frame our thinking in terms of search. Over time, search users seem to become more skilled in determining search terms and working with search engines (Howard & Massanari 2007), but it is possible that in doing so they are favoring the search orientation over other ways of thinking about discovery. For all the inaccuracy of the major search engines, there is something appealing in the idea that a few words can generate the information wanted. If someone wants to know more about making carbonated beverages at home, they could pick up a book or magazine article on the topic. But a quick web search will yield the information, often without context, but also without having to browse through that context. Does this mean that we treat inquiry as a kind of fast food: not very nutritious, but quickly delivered and satisfying?

At the same time, we should not ignore the rich diversity of content that is available on the web, and at least potentially available on search engines. In 2004, *Wired* editor Chris Anderson introduced the "long tail" phenomenon, drawing on an article earlier that year by Brynjolfsson, Hu, and Smith (2003) that described the success of online booksellers and other online retailers who provided a very large variety of products. A substantial part of the sales for these companies were obscure titles that a physical store would not bother to stock. No bookstore can afford to keep something on their shelves that may sit there indefinitely, but the volume of shoppers on, for example, Amazon.com ensures that even the most obscure titles are likely to sell eventually. Because they are able to warehouse many of their items, or have them drop-shipped from the publisher, they can provide a limitless selection with very little additional investment.

Obscure books, of course, have always been available. Any small bookstore is generally pleased to order a volume specially from even an unheard-of publisher. Amazon and other online retailers, however, also make these titles findable, and the result has been a shift in the market toward producing more for the tail. We might consider two counterweights. On one hand, there is the *New York Times* Best-Sellers List and Oprah's Book Club, acting as filters and providing consumers guidance on what titles are likely to appeal to them, since they seem to appeal to so many other consumers. On the other, there are the search and recommender functions of the online bookseller. Amazon.com might provide similar lists of best sellers, but rather than pushing everyone to buy the same set of best-selling books, it also has mechanisms that push buyers into the long tail. A recommendation system matches buyers to other buyers with similar tastes, and suggests books they may have missed. Individual reviews by readers also provide opinions that can quickly identify a niche product that has broader appeal. Unlike online book stores, the web at large does not have strong counterbalances to the centralizing forces of search engine rankings. There are portents that such a counterbalance is coming, most likely in the form of sociable search, but at present the largest search engines, and especially Google, dominate navigation on the web.

There can be little doubt that, at one level, search engines are contributing to a process that calls on us to understand the world in particular ways. This is particularly true of a growing transnational elite who are heavy users of information technology. During the 1990s, there was a growing feeling that the internet would create a new virtual culture, a cosmopolitan deterritorialized community that shared a new form of global knowledge. Not surprisingly, the creation of new space adds complexity to the issues of culture and local knowledge, rather than providing a ready-made solution (Robins & Webster 1999).

Cass Sunstein shares a story about visiting China and finding that his assessment of Genghis Khan was diametrically opposed to that of his host, mainly because of the differences in their education (2006, p. 217). The promise of a globalized, universal core of knowledge is that there is the potential for greater global cooperation when we share common ground on which to build. At the same time, there can be little doubt that search engines and related technologies of findability allow people to unite over fairly small interests and domains of knowledge. Young people who become obsessively knowledgeable about very narrow domains – often fanatical followers of sub-segments of popular culture – have taken on the Japanese label of *otaku* (Tobin 1998). The idea that there exists local knowledge in tension with universal understanding is not a new one. We will encounter this tension in other parts of the discussion of search engines, from interface design to public policy, but the nature of this tension is not easily discovered. Coming to an understanding of it requires us "to navigate the plural/unific, product/process paradox by regarding the community as the shop in which thoughts are constructed and deconstructed, history the terrain they seize and surrender, and to attend therefore to such muscular matters as the representation of authority, the marking of boundaries, the rhetoric of persuasion, the expression of commitment, and the registering of dissent" (Geertz 1983, p. 153). For now, it is enough to note that knowledge is at once universalizable and particular; that is, we are able to share, but not completely. Search engines promise to make that already complicated relationship even more complex, as they break through the friction of geography and affinity, forcing collisions between local and global knowledge.

Search and traditional knowledge institutions

The prototypical web search is often that of the scholar, academic, or student seeking authoritative knowledge on the web. The reasons for this prototype are varied. Many search engines have been developed by those working in academic settings. Moreover, the history of information retrieval has until more recently been closely tied to traditional libraries as authoritative repositories of knowledge. Libraries can be used to discover a wide range of information, both practical and scholarly, but do not reflect the full breadth of queries found on the web. The world of scholarship is not the sole source of knowledge for a society – far from it. Scholars have, however, for many centuries, been primarily involved in creating, storing, finding, indexing, and evaluating recorded work. It makes sense, then, when seeking out an understanding of search engines, to examine how these technologies are related to changes in academic research.

It is difficult to draw a clean line between the technologies that drive internet search engines and those used for library search, as they frequently draw upon one another. Some evidence can be found in citations of online materials in formal academic publishing, but even here, the fact that many scholarly resources are now available online, though not necessarily openly accessible, means that it is difficult to discern an online citation from a citation to a printed journal. A number of factors affect the decision to draw from online materials when doing research, including the availability of work online, and its accessibility by a given researcher. As long as a scholar has physical access to the internet, their self-perceived online skills are the most salient factor in determining the use of online resources (Y. Zhang 2001). Even once the more traditional barriers to using online work – access and skill – are overcome, it seems that there remain institutional and organizational impediments.

Search engines are derived from systems that have been used for many years to perform electronic searches of the literature from within libraries, or through paid services. Two of the largest and most complete indexes are the Web of Science and Scopus. These two indexes have a well-earned reputation for the reach of their indexes, the quality of the work they index, and the reliability of their citation data. Some universities base academic advancement on the citations found in the Web of Science, an indication of both its status in the academic community and the relationship of search technology to the institutionalized power of the academy. Today, it would be hard to imagine the same credence being placed in Google Scholar or Live Search Academic. Each combine the power of search engine ranking and filtering with search engines' concomitant weaknesses. There is something enchanting about the ease with which a search may be accomplished on Google Scholar, and its ability to quickly identify the most frequently sited articles on a topic. On the other hand, it is difficult to know just how extensive the Google Scholar record is, and what might be missing. As with Google's search engine more generally, the ranking algorithm is closed from public scrutiny, unlike some other commercial academic indexes. Finally, because it is drawing together a heterogeneous set of references, Google

Scholar tends to be plagued by repeated references, link rot, and layers of access protection. These flaws are enough to damn Google Scholar for many of those more familiar with citation indexing (Jasco 2005), but there can be little doubt that it has been widely embraced by many users who see it from the perspective of general-purpose search engines, rather than from positive experiences with traditional literature and citation indexes. As with search engines more generally, the question becomes whether commercial indexing services can survive when many of their clients are deserting them for the bigger, quicker, easier Google Scholar (Gorman 2006).

Putting professors in front of their computer screens instead of in the physical library hints at a larger shift, just as the move to the printed word did. Scholarship, as we understand it today, owes a great deal to the rise of the printing press and the libraries distributed around the globe (Eisenstein 1979). Victor Hugo haunts us: will the internet kill the university, at least as we know it? He had the advantage of hindsight when he wrote that "human thought was going to change its mode of expression, that the most important idea of each generation would no longer be written in the same material and in the same way, that the book of stone, so solid and durable, would give way to the book of paper, even more solid and durable" (Hugo 1999, p. 192). The university has traditionally served three functions, transmitting knowledge, storing knowledge, and creating new knowledge, all of which are quickly moving into the online world (Abeles 2002). Just as the library was the heart of the traditional university campus, the search engine has become central to the scholarly processes that occur online. What is now considered the physical university will, over time, be disassembled and distributed, with connections reaching out over the internet to draw learners into collaborative virtual and physical engagements (Halavais 2006). Such a far-reaching disruption of technological, social, and physical infrastructure cannot occur without some significant stress on existing institutions.

Chief among the challenges to existing hierarchies of the academy is the new demand for transparency and open access online. There is nothing about the internet that necessitates open access, and most universities continue to provide internet access to their paid, secure databases. However, there is a cultural imperative found on much of the internet that encourages the open sharing of information, and that imperative finds fertile ground among university faculties. Despite early efforts by universities to control access to scholarly materials on their servers (Snyder & Rosenbaum 1997), many large universities now provide fairly open indexing of their public websites. Many retain an intranet in order to protect their intellectual property and private information, but like other professions that communicate ideas, universities recognize the importance of gaining and accruing attention, and eschew gates and boundaries. Massachusetts Institute of Technology's OpenCourseWare project represents an obvious extension of this process, opening up syllabi, lecture notes, and other course materials to a public audience on the web (P. D. Long 2002). While the first step onto the web is a small one, it opens the door to more far-reaching changes.

Material that is on the web has the opportunity to be integrated more widely into the larger flow of writing and ideas. The early growth is centered squarely on scholar-centric sites that often represent a combination of search engine and archive. arXiv, for example, has revolutionized publishing in physics, changing the way in which physicists approach scholarly communication (Ginsparg 1996). CiteSeer has done the same for literature related to computing and information science. While these sites may fall under the label of "archive," they represent something more lively, something more akin to "professional working spaces" (Galin & Latchaw 1998). There was some early resistance to the transparency of the internet, and the open-access model of publishing, but there has been a sea change among faculty who are aware of open-access publications and willing to publish in them (Rowlands & Nicholas

2005). Scholars are exploring online in ways that move beyond publishing and accessing those publications, and in fields that might not be expected. It is hardly surprising, in some ways, that information science and physics have established themselves quickly on the internet, since the work of each already necessitates heavy use of computing. But these fields are being joined quickly by the social sciences, arts, and humanities. Patrick Leary (2005) writes about how historians of the Victorian era find their scholarly practices changing: "the eureka moments in the life of today's questing scholar-adventurer are much more likely to take place in front of a computer screen" than in the bowels of an Irish castle or over boxes in an attic. Open-access publishing becomes even more open, and visible, as search engines extract the contents of open-access journals and present them to a wider audience than closed journals could ever hope for (Suber 2007). Scholarly verticals like Google Scholar are particularly important here, since otherwise the academic literature, as a whole, would find it difficult to make its way into the public eye.

The ability to easily access and search the literature online is important, but each of these systems also provides the opportunity to explore scholarly literature in ways that have not until now been possible. There are certain affinities between citations and hyperlinks, and both undergird the distributed conversation that is at the heart of scholarship (Halavais 2008). Researchers have always made use of citations to explore backward through time to understand the development of a literature, but sites that collect citation data provide the opportunity for a scholar to move forward or sideways through that literature. Some of the information provided on a detail page for a Google Book Search – including key phrases, passages frequently used in other books, citations, and even a map of locations extracted from the text – presents us with a glimpse of ways in which scholars in the future might work their way through the literature. While it is still far from commonplace, automated conceptual analysis of the literature has led to medical breakthroughs, and has the potential of being expanded to other fields (Gordon, Lindsay, & Fan 2002).

The opening of this material onto the web also means that the walls and ivory towers of the university are far more permeable. Google Scholar provides no way of filtering results according to the traditional gold-standard of academic publishing, peer-reviewed journals, and does not (yet) rank the authors of these works. Of course, one could argue that the Google algorithms, as obscured as they are, represent a kind of peer review. Unfortunately, it seems unlikely that they are rigorous enough to stand alone as a filter, and they miss the beneficial impact good peer review has on revisions of an article before it is published. Nonetheless, the opening of material onto the internet has had a felicitous effect on the discussion of the efficacy of peer review, and a number of well-established journals are experimenting with various ways of opening up their peer review process.

The opening of the academy represents an opportunity for new kinds of balances between authoritative information. Traditionally, the institutionalization of knowledge has allowed for the creation of paradigms, the policing of truth, and agreements over commonly held beliefs. This practice – like that of the search engine – is exclusionary by design. Also like the search engine, academic institutions sometimes conflate authority over how we understand the world with other forms of political and economic authority. The diminishing power of the academic sphere does not, however, mean an end to that process of filtering knowledge. Search engines are taking on greater parts of that role, perhaps without some of the safeguards that have traditionally permitted a diversity of ideas in the academy. In practice, the structures of knowledge that were once the purview chiefly of professors are now shifting to technologies of knowledge. Traditional scholars will continue to be influential, in large part because they are able to attract an audience, but they will be joined by others who are able to do the same. It is natural that many scholars will resist this change, but the more appropriate reaction is to help to create safeguards that will allow for the continuing progress of knowledge. This is best accomplished by going to where knowledge is made and exchanged, and taking an active role in shaping the technologies that shape our discourse.

Academic institutions are perhaps the most important group undergoing these changes, from the perspective of accumulating and distributing knowledge. But all institutions work with knowledge and information, and all institutions are faced with similar demands for transparency and access. The kinds of questions that search engines force universities, libraries, and academic publishers to ask are being taken up by businesses and government organizations.

Addressing the imbalance

Umberto Eco's protagonist in *Foucault's Pendulum* writes "I had a strict rule, which I think the secret services follow, too: No piece of information is superior to any other. Power lies in having them all on file and then finding the connections. There are always connections; you have only to want to find them" (1989, p. 225). We would not want an entirely flat set of search results. Search engine ranking exists because there is a demand for it. Nonetheless, the rankings provided inherently reflect the status quo, and may not serve the collective interests well. Relevance is an intrinsically subjective notion, and the "generalized" relevance revealed in search engine rankings may have little to do with the relevance of an individual query situated within a very particular context and with a particular aim (Blanke 2005). As we have seen, most searchers are not sufficiently motivated to find the connections to relevant material if it is not provided to them at little cost to their attention. There are both reasons to counteract the role of the search engine as a technology that reproduces existing orders of authority, and ways in which this may be accomplished.

The problem of global monoculture is often assumed to be obvious, and it may be, but it is worth noting why it is something worth fighting against. Groupthink, at a massive scale, is only successful if it is always right. As a group, humans are fault-prone, and placing all of our bets on one cultural understanding or one course of action introduces a significant degree of risk. A lack of biodiversity allows for catastrophes like the Great Potato Famine, and a global monoculture risks the same kind of problems: there is no one right path for culture. On the other hand, there are real dangers in cultures unable to collaborate or exchange ideas. The difficult project of balancing cultural integrity with integration is central to the political project of multiculturalism (Parekh 2000). Likewise, for the larger issue of findability to be effective, we must recognize the rights of local culture not just to be represented, but to thrive, and those local groups must recognize that there are substantial global benefits for those who can translate their local practices into global practices.

Search tools are not innately homogenizing or authoritarian. However, ranking implementations that directly measure and reinforce authority are conservative in nature. It is not a question of whose power they conserve, but rather that they tend to enforce a winner-take-all structure that is difficult to break free from. As such, they comprise what Lewis Mumford (1964) called "authoritarian technics," those systemic tools that centralized power and control, "not limited by village custom or human sentiment." He went on to argue that these systems now constituted authority in and of themselves, without recourse to a human directing things from the top of the hierarchy. He argued not for an overturning of authoritarian technics, but to "cut the whole system back to a point at which it will permit human alternatives, human interventions, and human destinations for entirely different purposes from those of the system itself."

Although some have questioned the secrecy surrounding many search engines' ranking algorithms, it is not necessary to infer that the system is intentionally serving one group and not another. But, in a fitting metaphor, we might borrow from Langdon Winner (1980), who suggested that sometimes the technological deck was simply unintentionally stacked in favor of one constituency. For search engines, that constituency is generally those who have traditionally been able to command the attention of the mass media. There were complaints, both from journalists and from bloggers, about the amount of attention heiress Paris Hilton received in the United States during her brief incarceration for driving while intoxicated. Nonetheless, mass media and the networked media of the web seemed to give it equal weight. Broadcast media and search engines go hand-in-hand as powerful concentrators not of the collective will, but of the will of the majority.

The seeming coincidence between the agenda online and that offline may be somewhat misleading. There are millions of people around the world who had no interest at all in the scandal, but general-purpose search engines over-represent the central tendency. Just about anyone can create content for the web, but, as Introna and Nissenbaum (2000) tell us, "to exist is to be indexed by a search engine." That indexing alone is not enough. To return to the long tail of the bookstore, Google contains links to a reasonably large proportion of the web, but only a very tiny percentage of those links are made easily accessible to users. Accessing the deeper content of Google is as unlikely as accessing the deeper content of the web itself.

Gideon Haigh (2006) provides a compelling argument that Google is making us stupid by lulling us into complacency, providing a comfortable, convenient, and familiar service that we think we can depend on. That trust is a legacy of teachers and journalists who took their jobs as gatekeepers seriously, and we assume that Google is fulfilling a similar role. While Google dismisses the search engine's biases as natural outcomes of the ranking algorithm, Haigh argues we would never accept such an explanation from a human charged with providing accurate information. Whether these systems are actually making it easier to be uncritical, or whether they simply remain too difficult to use effectively (Brown 2004), the fact remains that the average searcher is probably finding less information, and less accurate information, than they should be, and they probably remain blissfully unaware that this is the case (Graham & Metaxas 2003). Search engines are a tool of unprecedented power when used appropriately, and a regressive system when the users become the used.

There are those who are "at home" on the web, and within the technological milieux of the internet; who are, as Prensky (2001) terms them, "digital natives." He uses that term to describe a generation of children who have grown up online, but in practice those children do not have the same process of inculcation of navigation skills in that online world. For some, search engines represent a part of their everyday experience, and work to connect them with a world that seems familiar. This feeling of belonging in a search-enhanced world is a result of, as Bourdieu suggests, "the quasi-perfect coincidence of habitus and habitat" (2000, p. 147). This coincidence applies particularly to a group of people, of various generations, who have been among the first to make heavy use of searching technologies, and who have become skilled at finding and evaluating information online. Those who are particularly able users of search have a special responsibility to find ways of restoring the balance of knowledge online.

There are several paths of resistance to the homogenizing process of major search engines. One alternative is to encourage competition among the top providers of search, moving from a handful of general-purpose search engines to scores. Unfortunately, the process of creating a general-purpose search resource is highly scalable and lends itself naturally to monopoly: one search to rule them all. In addition to the technology that initially brought the search engine to the top, Google has a particular set of advantages. Its visibility, verging on ubiquitous, as well as its familiarity and financial resources mean that it continues to win ever more adherents

(Sokullu 2007). Much of the discussion surrounding Google's supremacy does not ask whether the marketplace of search engines will expand, but rather who will usurp Google's position as search hegemon. The search engine that accomplishes this coup would need to not only deliver a superior search experience, but overcome the entrenched mindshare that Google enjoys, and would create its own entrenchments.

Rather than competing with the search oligarchy, one possibility is encouraging change from within the search giants. After all, the prototypical examples of companies opening up the long tail are not small organizations, but large corporations like Amazon.com, Wal-Mart, and Netflix. Indeed, very little encouragement is necessary, as some of the largest search engines have already recognized the need to draw links from the long tail and are providing structural access to it. Forays into non-commercial and scholarly search represent one example of this. Yahoo Research, for example, has an experimental engine called Mindset that allows the user to filter the level of commercial results on the fly by sliding an indicator more toward "shopping" or more toward "research." In fact, most of the niche vertical search engines provide access to results that may be pooled closer to the long tail. Taking this a step further, and drawing on the influence of a broader public, is Google's Co-op, which allows users to create their own vertical search engines and share them with others. Within a narrow area, this provides sites in the long tail a little "boost" onto the results pages, and with some fine tuning, and tagging by individual or group editors, it is possible to introduce even more differentiation (Biundo & Enge 2006). At least one group of researchers has suggested that random boosting of certain pages would act as a counter to the entrenchment of PageRank, and "reshuffle" the stacked deck (Pandey et al. 2005). As we shall see in chapter 7, the major search engines are also likely to continue to mine social networks in order to provide results that are less generalized.

Another possibility is to learn from the sophisticated approaches of the SEO industry, and attempt to reform the rankings of various websites through strategic linking. As long as there is going to be a hegemonic gatekeeper, one way of getting a message out is to exploit the filters of that system in order to reach a large audience. Googlebombing (or "link bombing") hints at this practice. Since Google gives great weight to the text within a link, a collection of links – particularly from popular websites – that contains similar text is likely to yield that page as a result. Clifford Tatum (2005) discusses two of the more well-known examples of Googlebombing: the association of George W. Bush's White House biography with the search term "miserable failure," and the effort to displace an anti-Semitic website as the first result for a search for "Jew." The two cases are interesting for different reasons. The efforts to Googlebomb the White House page yielded similar efforts to associate the "miserable failure" search with other politicians, in order to defend the current president. In the end, the effort to establish a connection was very successful, and suggested a way that Google could be collectively "gamed." The second Googlebombing was only undertaken after Google refused to remove the hate site from the search results, arguing that, while it was objectionable, the ranking algorithm itself was objective, and so the site was appropriately located on the results pages. Subsequently, Google apparently has changed the ranking algorithm to discount certain kinds of Googlebombing (Cutts, Moulton, & Carattini 2007).

Jakob Nielsen (2003) has suggested that one way of bypassing the power of established websites on search engines is by buying advertising or sponsored placement. Unfortunately, those who have money to buy their visibility on search engines are often the ones who have the least need. The commercialization of SEO means that, while almost anyone can publish a webpage, that page is likely to be relegated to the end of a list of search results. New forms of search literacy can help here, in order to offset the advantage of those who can afford the expertise of search consultants, but this may have only a limited effect on the disparity, since the SEO industry remains in place by keeping its practices esoteric and providing them only to the highest bidders.

If individuals cannot affect the structure of search engines, perhaps they can empower their governments to do so. In the following chapter, we will explore the possibility of a governmental check on search engine excesses, for example. Or governments may encourage the development of alternative search services, as the French have done. Quaero is an effort to create a more Eurocentric search engine, funded chiefly by the French government, with the aim of escaping the dominance of American search engines. While the development funds are dwarfed by the research budgets of the major search corporations, the history of search technologies suggests that when good ideas are supported, they can have significant effects on how people search. If nothing else, the Quaero project suggests recognition by national governments of the power of search; as Jacques Chirac noted, "Our power is at stake" (Meyer 2006).

Creating room for diversity, for conversation not smothered by the homogenizing force of a global index, is the ethical responsibility of the networked organic intellectual: the journalist, the librarian, the scholar, and the technologist, among others. They are charged, as William Blake had it, with the task of "Striving with Systems to deliver Individuals from those Systems" (1982, p. 154). As media have converged, these social roles have converged, and take on similar kinds of tasks. In each case, they are charged with communicating with the public, and, increasingly, with helping individuals in the public communicate with each other.

The search intellectual

What is needed is a level of information literacy that allows for effective use of search. Being an informed user of digital media means more than being a critical evaluator; it means that the person is a producer of media, a willing interlocutor in the distributed conversation of the web. Recreating search as a democratic technology requires a "leap towards digital authorship" (Vadén & Suoranta 2004), an authorship that understands the role of search and recognizes findability and making connections as central to what it means to create in a hyperlinked world. What is needed is a group of educators who have the skills necessary to understand search, and the ability to pass that understanding on to others.

A combination of technical skill, area knowledge, and conceptual acumen make up the searching elite. The best searchers understand what search engines are available, how each of them works, and what the strengths and weaknesses of each might be. They are equally aware of how to structure an effective query on a general-purpose search engine, how to use various forms of vertical search to mine the deep web, and how to find the people with appropriate area knowledge to help them when they are stuck. They may be able to locate expertise because of an extensive personal network, or by using social forums online. They are able not only to research a particular question as a single project, but to engage in continuous, real-time search, drawing in data on a topic automatically, fitting newly minted information into an emerging picture, and synthesizing a larger picture from the whole (Calishain 2007). Some of the most skilled users of search engines might even use them as tools to infiltrate computer systems, or to uncover military secrets (Long, Skoudis, & van Eikelenborg 2004). This set of skills is held by a relatively broad group, from intelligence analysts and private investigators to stock analysts and venture capitalists.

Some individuals are particularly capable of translating what they have found, and the means of finding it, to a broader group. This act of translation requires that they speak the language of the group they are serving, that they understand the cultural biases, and the metaphors that make search work for a particular group. This combination of skills and knowledge exists in what we might broadly call the "informing professions," journalists, librarians, teachers, scholars, computer professionals, marketers, public relations professionals, attorneys, and others. All of these groups are generally ethically obligated to help others to find information, though the professional codes may not directly address search engines. All searches provide some form of information that can become the basis for action. Less savvy and less educated searchers fail to understand the factors that influence the creation of hyperlinks, and the ways in which search engines exploit and are exploited by those hyperlinks (Hargittai 2008). It is the responsibility of more able searchers to help to inform their fellow citizens.

Knowledge is a vital part of democratic self-rule. Thomas Jefferson declared that "Whenever the people are well-informed, they can be trusted with their own government. Whenever things get so far wrong as to attract their notice, they may be relied on to set them to rights" (Jefferson 1903, vol. VII, p. 253). Wikipedia reminds us that there is value in the broad creation of knowledge by non-experts, but there is still room for experts. Although Jefferson was highly critical of the practice of journalism in his own day, calling newspapers "polluted vehicles" of information, journalists have a long history as agents of social change (McChesney 1996). John Dewey is often remembered for his work on newspapers and the "organized intelligence" of the nation. He believed the right kind of journalism, written by experts, could provide for informed discussion among citizens (Czitrom 1982). For Dewey, newspapers were eroding community ties and social capital (though he did not use that term), and so were the obvious target for reform. At the time, technology was blamed for the changes at hand, but Dewey suggested that instead it was a lack of understanding of how those technologies work:

> Only geographically did Columbus discover a new world. The actual new world has been generated in the last hundred years. Steam and electricity have done more to alter the

conditions under which men associate together than all the agencies which affected human relationships before our time. There are those who lay the blame for all the evils of our lives on steam, electricity, and machinery. It is always convenient to have a devil as well as a savior to bear the responsibilities of humanity. In reality, the trouble springs rather from the ideas and absence of ideas on connection with which technological factors operate. Mental and moral beliefs and ideals change more slowly than outward conditions. (1927, p. 141)

That was then, this is now, and not very much has changed. Once again, the technology that informs the public has changed more quickly than our conceptual or moral order.

James Carey argued that the changes in newspaper technology during the last century created the "new social role" of professional communicator: "one who controls a specific skill in the manipulation of symbols and utilizes this skill to forge a link between distinct persons or differentiated groups" (1969, p. 27). These brokers would work "vertically and horizontally," linking across social classes as well as those who were at the same "level" in the social structure. Carey goes on to suggest that this means the journalist takes on the role of an intellectual, translating discourse between communities. This calls to mind another description of the role of another intellectual of the people, Antonio Gramsci's "organic intellectual." The role of the intellectual for Gramsci (1957) is as a builder: someone who creates the scaffolding for collaboration and discussion, who translates between divergent "grammars" and unites groups. This organic intellectual diverges from the stereotype of the scholar in an ivory tower. Today's intellectual must "develop strategies that will use these technologies to attack domination and promote empowerment, education, democracy, and political struggle" (Kellner 1997).

Journalists are not the only professional communicators to take on this new intellectual charge; librarians also have a special role in helping people to understand the limits of search engines, and suggesting ways to overcome these limits

(Brophy & Bawden 2005). Many have suggested that the internet fundamentally changes the role of the librarian, but nothing could be further from the truth. The core role of a librarian is connecting people with the information that they need, and fostering the effective use of information resources (Noruzi 2004). The idea of the librarian is rapidly shifting from that of a person who collects and archives materials, to that of a person responsible for connecting people with information they can act on (Kane 1997). With good reason, many librarians have been critical of new technologies, and see search engines as threats. They are threats, but to libraries of the traditional mold, and not to librarians. The idea that knowledge is no longer bound by ancient walls, wooden shelves and bound volumes may be an aesthetic challenge, but the capabilities of librarians to organize, sort, discover, and disseminate knowledge are more important now than they have ever been. Librarians who are determined to fight against search engines, seeing them as a force for disintermediated access to knowledge, are fighting an unwinnable battle (Kenney 2004). Pandora's box is open, and the dominance of search engines today is likely to continue even as new approaches are taken.

Those who design search systems also have an ethical obligation to the communities in which they work. Computer professionals have the capacity to "be key agents in the redirection of computer technology to democratic ends" (Schuler 2001), and are in a position to encourage healthy debate, "helping a democratic populace explore new identities and the horizons of a good society" (Winner 1995). The stereotype of the computer programmer is that of a social recluse, someone without a clear social consciousness, a person who has taken on the characteristics of the machines she works with, and has no interest in tackling social problems. As Herbert Simon (1969) demonstrated in his classic *The sciences of the artificial*, there are close ties between the synthetic worlds inside the computer and the synthesis of policy "programs" that seek to solve a social problem. And this is hardly the first time we find computer systems that are reproducing existing social inequities, or that computer professionals are faced with confronting that ethical dilemma (Boguslaw 1971).

An earlier chapter addressed the importance of drawing users into the design process. Any designer hoping to have a popular service is likely to test the system on potential users and look for the features that are likely to attract new users. For the general-purpose search engines, this may mean a user model that is very broad indeed. While the company may find addressing the most general cases most profitable, there is also profit to be extracted by including the less common users from the long tail in the design process. Doing so may not just provide a new source of users; it may fulfill the ethical responsibility of an information professional to provide universal access. Universal access not only provides for the most common type of user with the most common kinds of skills, but recognizes the broad diversity of people who make use of a system (Shneiderman 2000). If a search engine works well for the average user, but systematically excludes, for example, older computer neophytes, it is important to understand the potential needs of this less numerous group and design alternatives for them (Dickinson et al. 2007).

Many of the problems with search can be addressed by search engines themselves, but doing so would require designers to recognize the shortcomings of their own systems and adopt a proactive ethical agenda. Engineers are notoriously unskilled at detecting the assumptions built into the technologies they design. John Law (1989) has argued that there is a need for "heterogeneous engineers" capable of considering the social, political, and economic dimensions of their work, in addition to the material outcomes. Some of the experiments general-purpose search engines are presently engaging in suggest, however, that they are aware of the problem of self-reinforcing hierarchies of ranking, and interested in mining the long tail of the web. There are technological solutions to the problem, particularly solutions that draw on social networks, and recommender systems like those used by the retailers who have exploited the variety found in the long tail (Gori & Numerico 2003), but technological solutions alone will not provide a more useful bias to a search engine. Although Google is responsible for the algorithm that represents the strongest example of such self-reinforcing hierarchies, in other ways it has demonstrated an affinity for some of the traditional values of librarians, at least relative to earlier search engines (Caufield 2005). We cannot rely on search companies as a whole to enact these changes. The long tail does not promise profits for search companies in the same way it does for retailers. Instead, what is required is an ethical commitment by the professionals working for these companies that goes beyond doing no evil. That is merely the first step.

The second step may be keeping fewer secrets. The competitive nature of the search engine business means that most advances are either kept under wraps, or patented, which results in power being further consolidated with search engine companies that have the resources to search. The recent advancement of open source search engine technologies provides some opportunity for search to be provided outside of the commercial framework. Some of these systems rely on peer-to-peer crawling and indexing, reducing the resources needed even further. Those search engines that open up greater parts of their search engines to public participation in design, public scrutiny in ranking, and public re-use of the resource are most likely to thrive in the new search environment. There are proposals in some countries to require search engines to open up the algorithms, and make clear how they rank results. There is value in such required disclosures, but it should be part of a larger embrace of access to knowledge and information.

Finally, there is a new kind of professional communicator that has taken on this role as search intellectual: the blogger. Certain blogs that manage to obtain large audiences can substantially upset the existing structures of authority on the web. By publicizing corners of the web that would otherwise remain out of view, they act as a counterweight to the hegemonic culture of the search engine. Slashdot, a site that covers technology news, represented an exemplar here, providing links to projects that were unlikely to be covered by mainstream news, and unlikely to be found in a simple search, at least until they were "Slashdotted." Today, the group blog Boing Boing, among others, performs a similar function, sweeping interesting bits from the fringes and periphery of the web into a central location where they are vacuumed up by readers eager to see beyond the mainstream choices on offer through the traditional news outlets and search engines. Once making an appearance on the site, of course, these pages are sometimes able to engage the circle of reputation and links that search engines tend to enforce.

From problems to issues

Search engines are our window onto the web world, and, without alternative views, it is not obvious when we see through that window darkly. It is extraordinarily difficult to gauge the social repercussions of the expanding use of search engines, but early indications are that it is changing how we acquire knowledge, and what knowledge means. Self-government requires that citizens are able to find relevant information, to actively seek out information from a variety of sources, and to engage in informed discussion. Search engines make it easier to find answers to specific questions, but can do so at the expense of the larger, diverse world of information and opinions. Unless countered with new kinds of search technologies, and new uses of the current technologies, we risk the internet becoming another anti-democratic, centralized medium, just the "latest blind alley" for those who hope communication technologies can be emancipating (Schiller 1996, p. 75).

Those who are skilled searchers command a particular amount of power in that they are able to locate and evaluate their information environment better than the average person.

That power provides them with a competitive advantage in the marketplace, as well as in the marketplace of ideas. Those with the ability to connect to a broader discussion have the responsibility to help others to do the same. "Search intellectuals" need not give up their own advantages, and need not abandon the capabilities of search engines that reinforce existing disparities, but they have a special responsibility to provide a counterweight, opening up discourses, and making sure that alternative voices are heard.

It is important that these search intellectuals are able to see the problems of searchers as more than merely individual problems. C. Wright Mills (1959) wrote about the relationship of individual problems to larger social issues, and the need to develop a "sociological imagination" that allowed for an interpretation of those social issues. The informing professions have a responsibility to develop that same sociological imagination, and to look beyond their narrow interests and help others to do the same. The problems of the individual are not the only indicator of social issues relating to search engines. As we have seen in this chapter, existing educational institutions and practices have had to evolve quickly in order to meet the challenge of a search-centric society. They have rapidly made changes in the way students learn and the way scholars do research. Likewise, traditional approaches to electoral politics are slowly adapting to the new search environment. The institutions that most clearly come into conflict with search, however, are those that have traditionally exercised control over the way in which discussions unfolded in the public sphere. Governments, and particularly national governments, have found managing search engines to be a challenge. What happens when the putatively natural, rational exercise of power by search technologies comes into conflict with the equally naturalized power of the state?

CHAPTER FIVE

Censorship

Google has found its informal corporate slogan – "Don't be evil" – to be more of a stumbling block than it had anticipated. Because, at present, it is the most visible and most utilized general-purpose search engine, its efforts to shape access to information have led to criticisms. The company has weathered censure for bowing to pressure by the Chinese government to filter search results, for bowing to requests by the US government to produce records of searches by users, and for presenting content to users (news stories, books, and images) without licensing the content. The core social question for a search engine is "Who sees what under what circumstances and in what context?" and in answering this question, political and economic battles are inevitable.

The argument over search engines is in some ways a recapitulation of the broader arguments of cyberlibertarians during the early 1990s. Riding on the profits of the dot-com bubble, there were suggestions that technology would usher in a new era of affluence, freedom, and leisure (Schwartz & Leyden 1997). By 1997, Eli Noam was already making clear that such utopian visions ignored the very real challenges that national governments were unlikely to overlook. "Thai child pornography, Albanian tele-doctors, Cayman Island tax dodges, Monaco gambling, Nigerian blue sky stock schemes, Cuban mail order catalogs," among other objectionable content, were not only inevitable, but would inevitably draw regulators of national governments onto the net.

Governments are most familiar with national borders, and so there was an early focus on ways of enforcing borders on the flow of traffic. Even if the internet is largely a distributed network, search engines are a common gateway for most users, and, as a locus of control, they quickly became a target of national police forces around the world. In the previous chapters, we considered how this control structure affects the commercial distribution of content on the web, and how it shapes exposure to balanced opinions. As it happens, these two forms of control come into very open confrontation in the case of search engine policy.

This chapter begins with a discussion about the shift from an international to a global system, the importance of networks to globalization, and the place of search engines in that process. We then go on to the most visible policy issue for search engines, and the one with the longest history, government-imposed censorship of ideas and discussion, imposed through search engines. After briefly exploring a particular subset of this censorship – relating to the search and discovery of protected intellectual property – we examine the other side: governments' attempts to acquire private information from search engines, and, in some cases, their efforts to make sure that information remains private. Finally, we explore some suggestions that governments should be more proactive in ensuring that search engines provide an equal footing for all content in order to create a healthy democratic discourse.

Gatekeepers and key masters

As noted in previous chapters, at their base, search engines perform as a global index. That word, "index," was first used in reference to books in the sixteenth century (indexes required the technologies of consistent printing and pagination), as an "indication" of where to find key terms in a book. The word had been used before this period also as a list of items that "indicated" something – most commonly, works that were not permitted to be disseminated.[1] Search engines perform a function analogous to switches in rail networks: they select and route information to the user. As such, they represent the latest in a long line of gatekeepers (Machill, Neuberger, & Schindler 2002).

Gatekeepers were once closely related to national governments. National public and private broadcasters often had cozy relationships with national governments, and, as a result, what the population was exposed to was shaped by media companies to conform to the ideals of the government. With technological changes, interactions around the globe are no longer routed through official channels. International relations now has little semblance to billiard balls bouncing off of one another, and more an affinity to spiders' webs, as individual actors, government representatives, and a criminal underclass all interact directly, without mediation from the national government or the national media (Burton 1972). This person-to-person global communication is facilitated by the internet.

Countries face a difficult choice when regulating content on the internet. If they are too open, it represents a challenge to the nation's ability to enforce moral or political order; if they are too restrictive, lack of access to the global knowledge market means a national economy that is unable to compete as effectively on a global scale (Benkler 2006). A number of countries have faced this dilemma, but perhaps none so acutely as Singapore. Singapore has had a history, since gaining independence in 1965, of strong police authority, particularly in matters of the press. Both printing in Singapore and distributing publications printed elsewhere generally require licenses, and have been carefully regulated for some time. At the same time, Singapore has traded on its reputation for having an open market and its history as a global entrepôt to drive its success in a global information economy. Seriously restricting access, as Burma and others had, would have meant economic suicide.

Instead, Singapore crafted a policy in the 1990s that let some things in, but carefully watched to see if users violated administrative policy. They accomplished this, in large part, by only allowing licensed internet service providers. The Minister of Communication at the time, George Yeo, likened Singapore's media policy to a cellular organism (1995). Cells have a semi-porous wall that lets in material important to its functioning, but shields it from threats. Rather than opening Singapore up to the net as a whole, he argued that there was a role for the government to play in controlling access. The hope was to balance internet access with the kinds of governmental control Singapore had exercised for decades. In this approach, Singapore differed from other national governments mainly in its degree of control. Many countries have national filters of one kind or another to stop material as it "crosses the border" on the internet,[2] and others control the content by punishing those who create or distribute certain kinds of materials.

The web provides a way of accessing documents, but search engines provide awareness. A filter can be counter-productive if a person knows that a page exists on the other side. In many cases, the search engine can actually provide a cached copy of the site, but even if this is not available, an enterprising internet user can often find ways around the filters if they know a document exists and want to see it. Creating a national filter but allowing access to search engines is a bit like a building a giant wall to keep things out, but leaving an unlocked door in the middle of it. Unless there is national control over that door, the wall itself has only a limited effect on the exchange of information. As the importance of search engines to web access has increased, national governments have become more interested in influencing how they work.

The most frequently cited example of such control is China's so-called "Great Firewall," which has acted as the technological arm of content-related internet policies in place in China since 1993 (Qui 2000). Like Singapore, China has been faced with a desire to maintain a governmental role as "editor," while continuing to encourage the growth of its economy. Their primary tool remains the use of filters that block access to particular sites (Zittrain & Edelman 2003). In 2002, China recognized that Google needed to be blocked, and, soon after, many web surfers attempting to reach Google were redirected to domestic search engines that were more directly under government control. The alternative was to extend its influence to the major search engines, like Google and Yahoo, in order to make sure that particular sites did not gain visibility. The Chinese government wanted to do what thousands of merchants had been unable to: affect the makeup of the search engine results pages. Search engines capitulated, while remaining characteristically cagey about the details, arguing that providing some search capability is better than none at all (McHugh 2003). Now results for searches on topics the Chinese government does not want its citizens discussing, from the Falun Gong movement to the occupation of Tibet, are filtered so that clicking on them leads surfers to a government page. In practice, this really is just an extension of the filtering process so that it is better able to manage the information Google and Yahoo provide, but there was certainly an appearance that, if not directly censoring for the Chinese government, Google at least provided assistance in showing them how censoring might be accomplished. Many were outraged at Google's willingness to adhere to the wishes of the Chinese government, especially during a period in which the company had resisted a subpoena from the US government requesting a large number of search histories.

The Chinese censorship issue is not the only case in which Google has faced criticism for adjusting (or not adjusting) results in order to comply with local wishes. In 2004, it came to the attention of American Steven Weinstock that a search for the word "Jew" on Google resulted in links to sites run by anti-Semitic groups, and he started a petition requesting that Google ban those sites from appearing (Becker 2004). At the time of writing, the second resulting site for this search on the original (US-based) Google.com is still "Jew Watch," a long-standing anti-Semitic site that seeks to reinforce negative stereotypes and hatred. The third result, as well as a "sponsored link" on the right side of the results page, both lead to an explanation by Google of why an anti-Semitic site is a top result for the search.[3] In the United States, Google has insisted that it will not go toward the slippery slope of interfering with the results of a given search query, and suggested that the high ranking for a site promoting intolerance is an artifact of their algorithm, as well as possibly a result of contestation over the current meaning of the word "Jew" (i.e., that it may now be considered a pejorative in English). The response, as noted in an earlier chapter, was a concerted Googlebombing campaign that brought the Wikipedia article on Judaism to the number one position.

At the same time, Google had quietly removed the result in countries where hate speech is not permitted; the site does not appear as a search result in France or Germany, where hate speech laws outlaw it. In short, Google is willing to interfere with its own technology when the linked material violates the law in a given jurisdiction, and have said as much in another case (Finkelstein 2003). The problem with such an approach is that, without transparency in either the ranking algorithm or the more human process of deciding what is excluded and where, there is always the potential for abuse and mistrust (Hinman 2005). Moreover, it seriously calls into question Google's hard line against "fine tuning" results, and raises questions of whether Google should censor in support of governments' political objectives, in cases where the censorship is more social (e.g. pornography), and in cases where they are protecting intellectual property (Rees-Mogg 2006). By creating local versions of their engine, Google is effectively providing a venue in which governments are able to regain their traditional role as censor.

Such censorship can have substantial public value. A number of countries have investigated search engines for inadequately distinguishing between sponsored links and organic results. At the time of writing, the Australian Competition and Consumer Commission has pursued court action to compel changes in Google's ad placements, and the

Federation of Consumers in Action in Spain has requested the government pursue the same issue with Google, Yahoo, and Microsoft (Tung 2007; "Google y Yahoo" 2007).

And restrictions are not limited to the traditional search products. Take, for instance, Google's response to government requests not to display certain areas on their mapping products. At present, Google Earth and Google Maps have pixilated Vice President Cheney's official residence and its environs, as well as blurring military sites at the request of the Indian government (Anderson 2007). Here, Google has abandoned the question of legality, and suggests that sites might be obscured under "exceptional" circumstances, which seems a bit too tautological to be a useful explanation. There are rational explanations for such exclusions; a plot was uncovered to plant bombs at New York's John F. Kennedy airport in 2007, for example, that had relied on Google Earth maps for planning (Buckley & Rashbaum 2007). In the aftermath, many have argued that expurgating potential targets on Google's mapping services has very little effect since the information is easily obtainable elsewhere (Bar-Zeev 2007; Harper 2007). But such a debate is moot, since there are no public criteria under which such exclusions take place, nor any easy or systematic way for observers to engage search engines to determine why exclusions have occurred, or to request that they be reconsidered. If we accept that some things should not be indexed, and other things may not belong at the top of the rankings, there should be some way for the public to learn that these decisions are being made and how they are made, at the very least. Better yet, search engine companies should engage in conversations with their users about what should and should not be excluded.

The reader probably does not need to be convinced of the utility of search engines, or of gatekeeping more generally. Society needs ways of filtering information, and as technology has eroded the previous filters that were forced on us – the effect of distance on the transmission of information, for example – it has replaced them with newly constructed information gateways. The question remains: who holds the keys to those gates? At present, both gatekeepers and key masters appear to be those who have traditionally held significant social power: media owners and political leaders respectively. To hold them accountable, we need a better way of gaining awareness of how they come to a decision.

Intellectual property

Search engines provide more than just search; they provide access to the intellectual labor of the world. Google's mission is "to make the world's information universally accessible and useful." Intellectual property laws around the world provide some degree of that power over access to the creators of intellectual goods. Given that search engines "indicate" the location of items that may be of interest to searchers, one might easily assume that the strictures of intellectual property are of little concern to search engines. In fact, the interests of major search engines are sometimes at cross-purposes with copyright holders.

Most search engines provide some form of a preview of the results for a search: Live Search Academic provides citation data for search results in a separate pane; Yahoo and Google, among others, provide a "cached" version of results pages and thumbnails of images found on the web; and many newer search engines provide everything from audio snippets to RSS feeds. Each of these has caused trouble for search engines. The largest search engines contain a repository of a large portion of the web that they usually have copied without the explicit permission of the creators, and without payment. In some cases, these collections are available to the public. Search engines are generally very responsive to requests to have items deleted from their caches, as are sites like the Internet Archive, which has caching as its primary function.

The question is whether and under what conditions a search engine can make use of some piece of the original work in creating an index of the web, and how much of that work they can present to a user as a guide to the content. As we have seen, search engines routinely retrieve and process the content of the web and other sources of information in order to try to provide an indication of what is available there. While there have been some attempts to legally restrict search engines from accessing information in order to index it – particularly in the case of Google's book scanning projects – most of the issues that courts have addressed were related to how much information search engines could reveal about the material they had indexed, and in what form. In the United States, much of this focus has been on the reproduction of images.

The Arriba Vista Image Searcher (which has been succeeded by the Ditto search engine: www.ditto.com) provided users with the ability to easily search for and save images found on the web. When it found an image it copied it temporarily, made a small, thumbnail version, and added it to its index. It also allowed users to optionally view a full-size version of the image, linked directly (inline linked) from the original site, and, at a later date, presented the resulting page in a frame. One of the sites the search engine indexed hosted photographs of the American West sold online by photographer Leslie Kelly, who sued Arriba for infringement. The decision by appellate court in 2003 on one hand established the use of materials for indexing as a fair use, but also put limits on that use. Thumbnail images, linked directly to the original work, were deemed to be a fair use of the material. The court found that the nature of the use, as well as the likelihood that it would help rather than hurt Kelly's photography sales, provided the grounds for considering it to be an accepted fair use. The inline linking of images from the original site, pulling them from their original context and providing for easy downloading, was not seen as protected by the fair use exemption, and Arriba Soft eventually paid damages to Kelly, based on this infringement.

The Kelly case established that, at least for the time being, the initial copying of materials in order to make an index did not represent an infringing use of the material. A later case, *Field* v. *Google*, extended this further in 2006, suggesting that text in Google's cache, which was made available to the user, was also subject to the fair use exception, since it provided a new kind of use of the material and, again, was unlikely to affect the potential revenues of the copyright holder. In a case currently making its way through the courts, Perfect 10, a producer of erotic photographs, has accused Google and Microsoft of copyright infringement, in a claim that seems similar to Kelly's. Perfect 10 claims, among other things, that because they sell thumbnail-scale photographs for use on mobile telephones, Google's and Microsoft's presentation of these thumbnails affects their ability to sell their copyrighted goods. They have also re-introduced the problem of frames and their ability to retransmit copyrighted work within a new context (Hartnick 2007). So far, the courts have rejected Perfect 10's claims, and have affirmed that thumbnails represent fair use.

Despite increasing alignment of copyright law around the world, the fair use doctrine, which provides statutory exclusions limiting the power of copyright, is not common in many legal systems, and search engines have encountered difficulty in working within various copyright regimes. Some have characterized copyright law, as it is currently enforced, as being antithetical to the operation of a search engine. Google, after a 2006 decision in favor of news service Copipresse in a Belgian court (Gibson 2006), noted that the suit "goes to the heart of how search engines work: showing snippets of text and linking to the websites is what makes them so useful" (Whetstone 2006). While producers of materials in the United States worry that search engines have too much freedom to make use of their materials, the relationship appears to be reversed in Europe.

The successful suit against Google in Belgium followed a similar Danish suit. In recent cases that appeared very similar to the Kelly case, German courts – while noting the finding in *Kelly* – reaffirmed the lack of any such clear protection under

German law. German courts made different findings in two cases: in one, finding Google guilty of copyright infringement, and, in another, finding that sites had given implied consent by not restricting access to their images using the robot exclusion protocol. The question of implied consent, as a defense, has come up in many of these cases, and some have argued that an effective solution may be to create a clear indication that copyright on the web is an "opt-in" sort of protection, requiring appropriate use of robot exclusion protocols and the like (see Allgrove 2007). However, attempts so far to extend the protections of the European Union's E-commerce Directive to provide clearer direction to search engines have faltered (Department of Trade and Industry 2006).

One of Perfect 10's other claims, and a claim that seems to come up repeatedly, is that search engines are linking to other instances of infringement, and thereby contributing to the pirating of their images. Again, search engines argue that, because they process millions of links each day, there is no way of effectively knowing whether the content on any of these sites is infringing. In 1998, the United States enacted the Digital Millennium Copyright Act (DMCA), intended to update copyright so that it would be more easily applied to digital communications, and to enact agreements reached within the World Intellectual Property Organization. It included a "safe harbor" provision for "information location tools," which would shield a website from lawsuits as long as they took down any material that infringed on a copyright or trademark after being notified of the infringement by the owner of that intellectual property. Although this may seem counterintuitive, linking to copyrighted work hosted elsewhere has been considered by the court several times to be a form of contributory infringement. Because search engines are unlikely to know the details of a copyright case, and because taking down a link frees them from legal liability, search engines are very likely to immediately comply with a DMCA "takedown notice," even in cases where there is little evidence of infringement (C. W. Walker 2004).

DMCA takedown notices are now a matter of course. The Chilling Effects Clearinghouse, a project supported by the Electronic Frontier Foundation and a number of law schools in the United States, attempts to track DMCA takedown notices, copyright suits, and other legal actions that may cause a chilling effect on free speech.[4] It lists 51 DMCA takedown notices in the first six months, all of them to Google properties. Google is not only the most popular search engine for web search, many of its properties support user-created media. YouTube, Blogger, and Froogle are told to remove links or subscribers who, according to the author of the takedown notice, are in violation of copyright law. Google began providing data about the takedown notices to the Chilling Effects Clearinghouse after what has come to be seen as an iconic use of the DMCA to quell criticism. In 2002, Google received a takedown notice from the Church of Scientology, requesting that they remove links to sites critical of Scientology. Despite wide criticism, Google complied with the request and removed links to the individual pages containing what the Church of Scientology claimed were infringements, but not links to the entire site. A search today on Google for "Scientology" yields a link to the protest site, Operation Clambake, as the fourth result.

The DMCA, of course, is a local law, and applies in theory only to the United States. Filtering, as a form of censorship, in France, China, or Belgium mainly affects the citizens of those countries, and there is room to argue that the citizens of a country, not search engines, are responsible for changing or maintaining the laws that encourage such censorship. But if the provisions of the DMCA are affecting users in other countries, search engines become another instrument of international power. Those who run a Bit Torrent tracker (a sort of search engine for distributed files) based in Sweden called "The Pirate Bay" routinely poke fun at DMCA takedown letters sent to them, as in a response to DreamWorks that read in part "As you may or may not be aware, Sweden is not a state in the United States of America. Sweden is a country in northern

Europe. Unless you figured it out by now, US law does not apply here" (Anakata 2004). While a takedown notice may have little direct effect when delivered to a foreign website, if a site does not appear in global search engines it is effectively invisible. The ability to have local filters installed in China or France avoids the problem of the most restrictive speech laws holding sway over the globe (Spaink & Hardy 2002), but it is equally disturbing if the concentration of the search industry in the United States means that US law predominates globally when it comes to search.

Search engines often fall back on the idea that the web is a new medium, and that the rules for that medium have yet to be fully written. Not surprisingly then, Google's effort to digitize several of the major academic libraries in the United States has led to contentious battles between the copyright owners (authors' and publishers' groups) and the search engine over who controls these works, and what privileges copyright provides. Google's position is that by scanning these works, indexing them, and providing a search interface, they are providing a new service – a service that is analogous to what they provide for material on the web. Google has argued that their book search, like their search engine cache, is protected under US law as a fair use (Baksik 2006).

An entire industry of authors and publishers relies on protection of their works in order to continue earning a profit from them. Someone writing a book twenty years ago would not even be able to have imagined the task Google has set for itself. These arguments often resolve to metaphors. As when a search engine visits a site on the web and makes a local copy of the material, the book scanning project necessitates scanning and making a new copy of the work of the author. The Authors Guild has argued that the first copy Google makes when it scans a book is a copyright infringement. The question is whether the court will see it this way, or as analogous to what Google already does on the web, and therefore permitted. If the courts see the analogy but find the copying infringing nonetheless, this could, Google's defenders argue, undermine the entire idea of a search engine (see Band 2006).

Siva Vaidhyanathan (2007) suggests that US courts are likely to see through this analogy, and that it is unlikely that the book scanning project will be seen as anything other than infringement, and that this could have an effect not just on the book scanning projects, but would likely roll back the fair use exceptions already provided by *Kelly*. He argues that "while the publishers' complaints are specious and overreaching, they might just have the law on their side," since Google will pretty clearly be making a copy of a copyrighted work in order to compile their index. If any patron made a copy of a book borrowed from the library, the infringement would be clear, and so it is clear in this case as well. Vaidhyanathan goes on to argue that the book scanning projects introduce significant concerns, particularly when combined with other Google projects. By tracking users, Google would have new insights into our reading habits. This transfer of cultural goods from relatively public to private hands is also concerning to a number of other critics. Even more concerning is that it might do to books what it has done to the rest of the web, ranking their importance according to a secret algorithm.

In Europe, authors enjoy an inalienable right to the material they produce, but in the United States control over content is frequently passed completely to publishers when a work is published. Neither authors nor publishers expected libraries to scan large portions of their collections, let alone that the globe's largest search engine would take on the project in cooperation with some of the largest libraries in the United States. Even if access to these books is limited to the equivalent of a hyperlink – a snippet of text with a reference to the book and instructions to go to the most relevant library – there will still exist the equivalent of one of the finest academic libraries in the world, scanned and under private control. (Another project, the Open Content Alliance, is working to provide an open archive of scanned books, and there are a large number of

similar projects working at a smaller scale around the world.)
Even if Google promises to never provide full text access,
things can change over time. The potential to deliver a library,
fully formed, anywhere in the world for little expense may
prove to be too tempting for the company at some point in the
future.

And it does not stop with indexing books. With its acquisi-
tion of YouTube, Google inherited another complex intellectual property challenge, though in this case the issue is not so
much links as complete or partial copies of video produced by
others. Google is presently negotiating contracts with the
largest owners of content licenses to allow for them to be
played on its service. The only intellectual property arena
Google seems to have avoided so far is music.

The ranking of search engine results presented by the
largest search engines is shaped by three types of policy: the
algorithms built by the search engine companies, the policies
of national governments, and the enforcement of intellectual
property rights (or threats of such enforcement) enabled by
new copyright laws. Censorship is just another word for filtering, and we rely on search engines to filter our results. It is
important to understand that these filters, while they are generally not manipulable by individuals, remain subject to those
who have traditionally wielded social power.

Promoting search diversity

It would be wrong to assume that copyright holders and
national governments alone limit the results of major search
engines. Certainly, the engineers who create and modify the
algorithms used by each search engine exercise substantial
control over the process, identifying cases where the existing
algorithm is not producing expected results, and redesigning it
so that it performs more closely to expectations. At least in
Google's case, it also seems that the hesitancy to blacklist individual sites, except when there are legal grounds for doing so,

does not stop search engines from blacklisting sites they feel have taken unfair advantage of their ranking process.

In 2002, a search optimization company called SearchKing created the "PR Ad Network," an attempt to build the PageRank of several companies by linking them to one another. Those who create websites knew then, as they know now, that achieving a high rank on Google's results pages was accomplished in large part by encouraging incoming links. Although the sites may not have been related, interlinking helped their position on the charts -- for a time. Then both SearchKing's ranking and that of its clients began to drop precipitously. SearchKing sued Google, and refused to drop the suit when its ranking was restored. Google successfully defended against the suit, arguing that they had the right to determine their own rankings, including blacklisting companies like SearchKing. An article in *Slate* summed it up thus: "More than anything, the suit proves that when you pit the questionable virtue of an Internet parasite against the dubious integrity of an Internet monopolist, you're left with a case that makes everyone just a little bit nauseous" (Lithwick 2003).

This was hardly a unique case of punitive blacklisting. More recently Google blacklisted the German websites for BMW and Ricoh because they felt that the sites had sought to mislead the search engine (Miles 2006). In each case, Google alone made the decision, and there was no clear avenue for appeal. Google makes clear that it disapproves of search engine optimization, but, as we have seen in a previous chapter, the line between spamdexing and simply creating effective information design is not always as clear as we might hope. If I change the titles on my blog to list the subject before the blog name in the title, is that unfair manipulation, or just making clear what the topic of the posting is? If I leave my website address in the comments of blog posts on other blogs, is that a form of link-spamming, or am I just an active commenter? Google knows well that a high ranking on its search engine commands a certain value (it is, after all, value that also accrues to Google itself), but at the same time forbids website creators from actively pursuing that value.

The interventions by governments mentioned thus far are intended to restrict the flow of particular classes of information, but there is at least the potential for governments to play a different role. Given the importance of an informed citizenry to effective government, there may be an interest in countering the hegemonic tendencies of search engines, and encouraging more open discourse. For much of the last century, media outlets in the United States were required to provide equal access to opposing positions. The idea was that because newspapers and television broadcasters had special access to the living rooms of Americans, they should be responsible for providing a balance of ideas. This justification for interference in privately owned media was largely removed when in 1974 the US Supreme Court ruled that the *Miami Herald* had the constitutional right to publish the political opinions of its choice and that a Florida law demanding equal time for alternate views violated the newspaper's speech rights (*Miami Herald Publishing Co.* v. *Tornillo*, 1974). The tradition of state management of the airways, and of the cultural heritage of the nation, remains far stronger in Europe and in many other parts of the world.

Given the even greater ability to distribute ideas online – just about anyone can create a website – it would appear that there is even less need for government intervention. But the ability to create media matters little when the ability to find those publications rests with a very small number of search engines. Of all searches in the United States, 64 percent are currently made on the Google search engine, and Yahoo, Microsoft, and Ask make up an additional 34 percent of searches, according to Hitwise (2007). The other 49 search engines Hitwise tracks accounted for only 1.68 percent of searches. Under those conditions, it certainly seems like there is something approaching monopoly or cartel control of search. If the companies who are handling the searches were open about how they ranked results, that might not be a concern, but because they control the vast majority of search functionality on the web, they deserve to be carefully scrutinized.

Some suggest that the most damaging biases, the retrenchment of current inequities and "winner-take-all" search, are best met with technological solutions, especially personalized search. Engineers generally support the idea that this is a kind of "bug" and something that will be changed with the natural progression of technology: that, as Eric Goldman (2005) has it "technological evolution will moot search engine bias." Goldman's rosy assessment is that, as personalized search becomes more capable, it will break up the unitary nature of global search, and there will be as many winners as there are people searching. The only problem with this, he suggests, is that it may lead to intellectual isolation of the sort described by Sunstein (who, ironically, sees the serendipity of search engines as a counterweight to the atomization caused by personalized filtering; 2001, p. 206). If history is any guide, there is a tendency for just the opposite to occur, and for communications technologies – particularly those controlled by monopolies and oligopolies – to become more centralized. Political and economic forces both favored such centralization, though recent changes in niche marketing may diminish some of the economic desirability of the "one size fits all" service.

Goldman is right, however, in his core argument: that search engines are biased because that is their intended function. Rather than personalized search, sociable search aims to provide a middle ground for avoiding either centralization or atomization, and the direction of the industry suggests that there is an economic impetus to move toward sociable solutions. But it is unlikely that this will occur at the expense of continued domination of search by a handful of companies. Even as search becomes more complex, there will always be the need for general-purpose global search engines, and, with them, the need for social and political checks on their power.

Pasquale & Bracha (2007) have proposed a solution that relies on federal oversight of the industry. The early utopian thinking about the internet as a place where anyone could become a pamphleteer has given way slowly to a reality that – while still supporting an amazingly diverse assortment of content – seems to be gradually converging toward points of control. After reviewing some of the common arguments on both sides, the authors suggest that – in order to protect democratic discourse, ensure economic competition, promote basic fairness, and avoid deception – the search engines need oversight. They endorse a "Federal Search Commission" that is able to investigate claims of bias. They acknowledge that there are legitimate reasons for maintaining secrecy, in order to thwart SEO efforts, and that it might be possible to create something similar to the US court charged with secretly hearing national security surveillance matters, the Federal Intelligence Surveillance Act (FISA) court.

There are less extreme solutions that still do not require an entirely *laissez-faire* approach to governing search engines. A more palatable solution might be a quasi-judicial agency like the Securities and Exchange Commission which, particularly with the addition of the Sarbanes-Oxley Act in 2002, routinely deals with balancing corporate desires for secrecy with the public's right to know. Perhaps a small nod to earlier fairness approaches would require a "right of reply" so that those who dispute the results of a search have a space to present their case and perhaps discuss it (Weinstein 2007). Google has already taken interesting steps in this direction, by allowing the subjects of news articles that appear on Google News to reply to stories that include their name. Google's contribution to the Chilling Effects Clearinghouse also suggests a move toward opening up a discussion over the forces that shape the results it produces. At a minimum, there needs to be a concerted effort to make users aware of the sources of bias in search engines so that they can account for this bias when they search.

Other countries' approaches to regulation at this point provides little guidance. The heavy-handed censorship of China, Singapore, and dozens of other countries does not provide a model that allows for equality or access. In practice, because a number of the most popular search engines in the world are owned by American companies, the solutions taken in the United States will inevitably have global repercussions.

Don't be secretive

Google has been perhaps unjustly criticized for its unofficial motto "Don't be evil," but the phrasing of that motto is telling, particularly in light of their recent difficulties in interacting with the governments of China and the United States. Some have criticized the lack of sophistication in that motto, and no doubt Google is finding that it is not always clear how to avoid being evil (Argenti, MacLeod, & Capozzi 2007). It is important for a search engine that is the gatekeeper for much of the world's communications to understand that it is not necessary to *be* evil in order to *do* evil. Sometimes structural inequities and technocratic decisions that may be perfectly rational and lacking any harmful intent can nonetheless lead to problems in the human systems that make up the web. The safest way to avoid doing evil is to be as open as possible about the decisions you make as an organization and why. Google needs to raise the bar beyond avoiding malevolence, and take on the ethical responsibility of the global mission it is seeking. While the fact that it is answerable to its stockholders and demands for an ever-increasing share price may place an upper limit on how much trust it can accumulate, it can do far better than it has in crafting a social contract with its users.

That will not end the scrutiny, nor should it. Google-Watch is a website dedicated to explaining what is wrong with Google, from convoluted conspiracy theories to cogent complaints about process, but it stands out against a public that has an unreasonable and unwarranted degree of trust in its search engines and its own ability to use them. Google, who has embraced the long tail and open transparency of blogging and of user-created media, has to demonstrate its trust of the public if it hopes to retain that trust itself. Transparency comes with its own dangers and potential costs (Grimmelmann 2008), but just as we seek transparency and openness from our governments, we should expect something similar from the search engine industry.

CHAPTER SIX

Privacy

The traditional view of identity in cyberspace is that it extends the trend of metropolitanism and cosmopolitanism: we simultaneously inhabit multiple selves and can easily step into alternative identities as we appear online. In contrast, search engines have thrown us back into village life in many ways. Public identities are often constructed out of what may be discovered via a search engine, and this affects how we view our colleagues, our friends, and our family members. Drawing heavily on the burgeoning exhibitionist technologies like blogs, social networking sites, and photo-sharing sites, search engines help us to create portfolios of the people we interact with. In many cases, this means that they provide us with information on parts of their lives that would otherwise remain hidden, at least to most of the world.

The capacity for accumulating these profiles encourages their use, and goes hand-in-hand with a shift in what we consider private information. More of our private lives are open to surveillance today than in the past, and individuals are able to make better use of information that may be found in the public sphere. Yochai Benkler (2006) draws on several examples of this new watchdog function, including the distributed investigation of the Diebold voting machines. These new conceptions of how privacy works is reflected in the language that is used to discuss it; "dataveillance," "sousveillance," and "reciprocal transparency" all suggest that privacy is far from a unidimensional concept (Clarke 1988; Mann, Nolan, & Wellman 2003; D. Brin 1998). Search engines will continue to play a role in determining the future of privacy, but also in the creation of self-conception, and a new public record of the "webs of group affiliation," as Simmel (1964) termed them.

Mark Poster (2006) links the rise of identity theft to the new transparency of the internet, a transparency encouraged by search technologies. Identity, from the perspective of such thefts, is "not one's consciousness but one's self as it is embedded in (increasingly digital) databases. The self constituted in these databases, beyond the ken of individuals, may be considered the digital unconscious" (p. 92).

Reputation management

In the film *The Jerk* (1979), the title character, played by Steve Martin, is excited when he finds his name in the telephone directory: "Page 73, Johnson, Navin R. I'm somebody now. Millions of people look at this book every day. This is the kind of spontaneous publicity – your name in print – that makes people." No doubt many people had the same reaction when they first searched for their own name on a search engine, and it generated a link to a site that was actually relevant. These days, it is rare for someone not to appear by name somewhere on the web, but appearance on a search engine seems to put a person on the global stage.

Self-Googling, personal brand management, ego-surfing – all describe the act of monitoring one's own image as reflected by the major search engines. Excessive self-Googling may reflect a certain vanity, but finding out how others perceive you is a natural impulse, as is the temptation to shape that image. In 1956, Erving Goffman (1997) described this activity as "impression management," a term that is still often used among psychologists. Some find the overt concern over managing one's impression unseemly, and others think it is vital. In either case, it seems that, from fairly early on, the web was seen as a place for creating and distributing that impression (Erickson 1996). Tom Peters (1997) argues that "our most important job is to be head marketer" for our personal brand. In fact, in this age of search engines, there are companies that specialize in protecting our online reputations (Kinzie & Nakashima 2007). Checking for one's name in a search engine provides a glimpse of what others might see and, since search engines often influence others' opinions of us, or even provide a first impression, it is important to know what kind of picture a search portrays. That image is inevitably incomplete and disjointed, emphasizing certain features while ignoring others.

The cultural currency of using Google to find out about someone is reflected in the neologisms that surround the practice (McFedries 2003). The relationship of Google to identity is also reflected in online games built to reflect the information found on the search engine. Googlism is a site that simply collects information from websites found on Google using the "____ is ____" pattern to describe people, places and things. Entering a name like "David Bowie," results in phrases like "david bowie is god" and "david bowie is to release an album consisting entirely of instrumentals," along with several dozen others. Google Fight graphically depicts the number of hits for each of two terms, so that you can determine the winner between, for example, "pen" and "sword" (pen wins). There is a natural assumption that the number of Google hits a name receives corresponds in some way to the popularity of that person (Bagrow & ben-Avraham 2005).[1]

A serious strain underlies this playfulness. A survey of executive recruiters found that more than three-quarters used search engines when screening applicants, and more than a third had eliminated a candidate from consideration based on information they found as part of that search (Mayclim 2006). The recruiting process, and any other process that involves trust and potential partnership, requires a reduction of uncertainty. Rituals have evolved around the process of uncertainty reduction, the process by which we gradually reveal ourselves to strangers. Search engines change those rituals, providing a way of finding out about someone without engaging in the ritual dance of conversation (Ramirez et al. 2002). It remains to be seen how exactly this affects the way people establish and maintain friendships. However, there are problems with what we reveal to others online.

First, names are very rarely unique, and it can be easy to mistakenly assume that the pages called up by a search engine are all about the same person. Even a search for the very common name "John Smith" on Google yields information about the founder of Jamestown, Virginia, a researcher at IBM, and a British folk singer. Someone looking for information on one of these Smiths would likely be wary, because the name is so common, but it is all too easy to conflate the people returned as results. Since people are far less likely to encounter other identifiers in the text along with the name (say birthdates, telephone numbers, or other forms of identifying information), it can be difficult to disaggregate the results, particularly for someone you do not already know.

This has led to the phenomenon of "Google twins," people who become obsessed over others who share their name on search engines (Heyamoto 2007). It is sometimes amusing to see what you "might have been," or what others are likely to find (erroneously) when they try to learn more about you. It is also sometimes awkward. Many of my graduate students have encountered difficulties with what employers discover on the web when they go out onto the job market. One of my graduate students discovered that she shares her name with an adult films actress. Although she has never been questioned about this, she worries that people may search for her name and be confused. Since there is no easy way to bring up the fact that one is *not* a porn star, without raising even more concerns, she is left with the possibility that her "twin" leads to others prejudging her, for better or worse.

The other possibility is that search engines may reveal material that is related to you, but does not put you in the best light. There have been several highly publicized cases of people writing things on public blogs that reflected poorly on their employer. Once the employer discovers the writing, the employee is "dooced," or loses her job because of the post, a term named after a particular case (Twist 2005). This bad publicity might never have been discovered if not for the ability to search by a person's or company's name. Sometimes someone's past can come back to haunt them through a search engine, bringing to the fore youthful indiscretions, or choices that seem particularly bad only in retrospect (Swidey 2003). One former student emailed me requesting that I help him to remove a blog he had created while a graduate student; in the hiring process a company he was hoping to join had discovered that he had criticized one of their major clients. However, once material is out on the web, it can be extraordinarily difficult to remove, particularly if it is interesting enough to save. It may be cached or archived in various places around the web, so removing it from the original site may not be enough.

Increasingly, the problem material may not be anything you posted. It is now common to post photographs publicly, and often to identify the people in the photographs. After a wild party, you may find images of you are available online. Because image search remains in its infancy, that need not be a problem until someone "tags" the photograph with your name, helpfully making it findable by anyone searching for your name on the web. Someone may have less than flattering things to say about your talk at a local library, about the quality of what you sell on eBay, or about your fitness as a mate. As amateur genealogists move online, they may connect you in familial webs that you may not have wanted the rest of the world to know about. And sometimes it is material that existed before in other forms, but that has become digitized and searchable. The *New York Times* recently opened their archive to the web, and, as a result, they are receiving daily complaints about embarrassing articles that are now far more accessible than they have been in decades (Hoyt 2007).

Identity theft is much easier when so much information can be discovered from a few web searches. The kinds of questions that have traditionally been used to ascertain identity – things like your mother's maiden name, or the name of your pet – are now often found on search engines. If they are not available there, searches of public records and private databases also contain this previously "private" information.

Searchable digital identity is a two-sided sword. For all of these dangers, there are still good reasons to be easily findable online. By making it easier for people to meet you and by making clear what your interests and desires are, you have the potential of finding people who share similar interests. One of the reasons recruiters search the web is that a search engine can collect documents from a range of sources, which provides a more trustworthy picture of the individual.

The words we post now present us not only to the world today, but also to the future. As new university graduates find their Facebook profiles scrutinized by potential employers, they may become concerned that their online persona does not reflect their real capabilities. In a decade, that photograph of them drunk at a party will still haunt them. Throughout the book we have hinted that projects like the Internet Archive are a form of search engine, as they collect and store data from the web that can then be searched by keyword or browsed by date. By storing peoples' history, internet archives create a people's history, a record of how not-so-great men and women thought and wrote. But other search engines, by accessing the wide range of documents on the web, also create personal histories. The fact that these histories may be a bit jumbled (ZoomInfo lists 21 of my employers, of which only 2 are accurate) only makes matters worse. And as search engines expand their breadth and capabilities, more history – which may already exist in electronic form somewhere out on the web – will become findable.

The trajectory of personal information Google has acquired provides a hint of what the future may bring. When Google obtained an archive of Usenet postings, many found their preweb personal histories suddenly made more public in a postweb world. Likewise, as photographs in Flickr and Facebook are tagged to indicate that a particular person is in them, they become a searchable part of a history that may already have been online, but was previously not linked by name to an individual. In the near future, much of that process may become routine, with photographs and videos being automatically tagged with recognized faces – and the inevitable errors that come with that process. Much of the use of our name online is entirely outside of our control.

There are advantages to being able to move past your own history. Many people encounter times in their lives when they are ready to leave the past in the past, make a clean break, and start over. Some of these changes are so common that they are almost ritualized. When many people make the transition from high school to university, they deliberately leave behind the personality and personal histories they had in high school. With a new set of peers, and often a new city, university provides people with a chance to reinvent themselves. Already, with Facebook and other social networking sites, this process has become more difficult. As search engines pervade most of our lives, it will be difficult to leave personal histories behind, at least without changing your name.

Your search is showing

In August of 2006 AOL publicly released data from a three-month period so that researchers could make use of it (Arrington 2006). It contained the search history of over 650,000 users, collected at random. The intent was a good one: by providing a massive database of queries, it was possible to gather how and why people searched for items. Usernames had been stripped from the data and replaced with numbers. Under immediate and heavy criticism, the data were removed from the site three days later, but it had already been downloaded and made available on other sites. The scandal eventually led to the resignation of AOL's Chief Technology Officer and the researcher responsible for the release of the data (Zeller 2006).

The release provided a great opportunity to ask the question: how much is revealed by what we search? Particularly when the names of the searchers were concealed, could it even be claimed that there was a violation of privacy? Within hours, people around the web were picking out patterns. Within days, individuals had been identified and intriguing examples of search streams had been extracted. Some of these were disturbing. For example (McCullagh 2006):

> *replica loius vuitton bag*
> *how to stop bingeing*
> *how to secretly poison your ex*
> *how to color hair with clairol professional*
> *girdontdatehim.com*
> *websites that ask for payment by checks*
> *south beach diet*
> *nausea in the first two weeks of pregnancy*
> *breast reduction*
> *how to starve yourself*
> *rikers island inmate info number*
> *inmatelookup.gov*
> *www.tuportal.temple.edu*
> *how to care for natural black hair*
> *scarless breast reduction*
> *pregnancy on birth control*
> *temple.edu*
> *diet pills*

Copies of the database ("mirrors") are still available, and some allow for the rating, tagging, and discussion of interesting search histories.[2] An article in the *New York Times* detailed how it tracked down one user, a 62-year-old widow from Lilburn, Georgia, based on what she searched for. When alerted to the trail of searches that had been recorded, she said "My goodness, it's my whole personal life. I had no idea somebody was looking over my shoulder" (Barbaro & Zellner 2006). The article notes that, like other search histories, this one was a "catalog of intentions, curiosity, anxieties and quotidian questions."

John Battelle (2005) refers to Google as a "database of intentions." We search for things we are hoping to know, hoping to do, and hoping to become. It is the most powerful unobtrusive measure of collective and individual desires that society has ever known. Google has capitalized, to a certain extent, on the aggregation of that data. By watching what searches are becoming more popular, Google is able to gauge the global consciousness directly. If tens of thousands of people are suddenly searching Google for the same person or issue, it is a pretty good indicator that there is a consensus that the keywords describe something interesting. It does not tell you why they are interested, but mapping the attention alone is powerful. Google first provided summaries of this aggregated data in a report called the Google Zeitgeist, ranking the searches in various thematic ways. Zeitgeist has given way to Hot Trends, a list of the fastest-gaining searches, but without the minimal level of analysis Zeitgeist provided. Google Trends itself allows you to chart attention over time, and compare politicians, products, or ideas. To draw on an earlier example, it is possible to plot "pen" against "sword" to see what people are searching for. "Pen" wins here as well (in large part because of politician Jean-Marie Le Pen's appearances in the news), but the trend will clearly put "sword" ahead in the near future. Google provides more information about the current trends in their television program *Googlecurrent_*.

Google also uses search histories to profile individual users. This allows them both to personalize search and to deliver targeted ads. Google has recently made search histories available to registered users, so that they are able to re-find items located in previous searches. These profiles support collaborative filtering, though it is invisible to the user, and Google suggests you probably will not notice it in your normal searching. Google argues that, with personalized search, you get more of the things you are most interested in. It also means that sponsored items, the targeted marketing that appears on the search engine and elsewhere on the web, will better meet the interests of the user.

The search history function also allows those who are logged in to delete their search history completely or in part. The obvious assumption is that the profiled material would then be deleted, but there is no explicit word from Google on this. They track users who do not log in, placing a cookie on their machine to be able to identify them each time they return. The search results may no longer be associated with the user's account if she deletes her search history, but Google may still be tracking her.

Google has the capability of tracking users even further than search. Because Google advertising appears on many websites, and many websites make use of Google Analytics (a free tool for analyzing traffic to a site), there exists the potential to track users as they move around the web. DoubleClick, one of the first web advertisers that placed ads across multiple sites, did just this. Naturally, each could only detect user activity on sites where they had placed advertisements, but as more and more websites hosted DoubleClick ads, it was possible to map users' moves across these sites. This provided DoubleClick a valuable source of marketing data. And now, Google is seeking to acquire DoubleClick, though there are efforts being made through the regulatory agencies in both the United States and Europe to keep this from happening. And it does not stop with web search: as Google either innovates into new areas or acquires existing services, new sources of behavioral information are created. The list of applications and services offered by Google today is staggering and nearly all-encompassing. It would be entirely possible to communicate and conduct all of your business without ever leaving the warm embrace of Google. And the company shows no sign of easing up, moving into infrastructure, mobile services, and traditional broadcasting.

Given this concentration of private information, it is natural to question Google's actions and policies. In the past, Google has been criticized for using cookies that did not expire to track user activities, for tracking email content in a way that was not transparent to the user, and for a number of other transgressions. Efforts to personalize individuals' experiences with the search engine and Google's other services mean creating an electronic dossier that is exceptionally detailed. Indeed, Google's CEO, Eric Schmidt, has suggested that a more complete profile of users is at the heart of the company's rapid expansion, and Yahoo and other search engines are also seeking that enhanced portrait of the people who visit their sites (Daniel & Palmer 2007). More recently, Google has attempted to become more transparent, and has taken steps to limit the collection and retention of certain private information, but as much of our lives move online, and we increasingly find ourselves among suites of applications from one of the search oligarchs, we see a concentration of private information like no other. Although Google says that they have no intention of combining data from all of these sources (including DoubleClick) into a single profile, the concern is that nothing outside of this intent would stop them from doing just that (Edwards 2007). If we continue down this path, Google will know more about you than anyone else does, including yourself.

Even if Google does not collect that data into a single profile, there is the added concern that the US government might. Several years ago, there was a great deal of concern over a project that went under the name of "Total Information Awareness," and sought to combine multiple sources of data to track and predict domestic threats. The project was scuttled under public scrutiny, but the elements that make up information awareness are still actively pursued (Harris 2006). There really is not another option; for governments to lead effectively they need to be collecting, combining, and filtering all the information they have access to, just as any organization must in the networked world.

And governments want access to the valuable data search engines collect. When the US government requested two months' worth of search logs, Google was unique in fighting the request; other major search engines acquiesced (McCullagh & Mills 2006). Although the existence of such records and a willingness to provide them to the government is troubling, it is not entirely surprising, and fits with the history of close ties between US communications companies and the US government. Government monitoring programs like Shamrock and Echelon worked largely through the collusion of communication companies (Bamford 1983; Singel 2006).[3] Perhaps the unusual element of this case was that, because it was not tied to national security, the public actually heard about it.

It also came at a time when search engines had already made news on the public stage for their interactions with the Chinese government. Google had just reached some form of an agreement that allowed Chinese citizens to reach the Google search engine, but not to use it to research topics the government found too controversial. Microsoft had succumbed to pressure from the Chinese government to shut down the blog of a dissident. Yahoo provided information to a Chinese court that allowed a dissident, Shi Tao, to be sentenced to prison for ten years (Zeller 2006). These acts have led many to question whether privacy is appropriately placed in the hands of national policy. Google has responded by urging the creation of coherent and coordinated international policy on privacy (Ljunggren 2007). While certainly a laudable goal, handing the problem over to national governments is irresponsible; these companies should abide by a set of ethics that rises above national policy (Fry 2006). Though it is, as Google's Elliot Schrage told the US House of Representatives in 2006, an "imperfect world" that requires "imperfect choice," Google and other search engines should be as prepared to fight for their customers as they are to fight for approval of their corporate acquisitions.

If Google is already at the center of such flows of information, it represents the ultimate target: a treasure trove of private information. The threats to that information are varied. Google might, through some unforeseeable error, accidentally leak that data to the public. Identity thieves may find a way through Google's security. The profiles would be amazingly valuable to anyone who wished to be able to match a set of intentions to a group of people. Anyone who has anything to sell would love to have access to such data, as would many governments. Google has taken the step of anonymizing their logs for those who are not signed in, providing a small measure of protection. But given the potential of this compiled set of dossiers, it seems unlikely that Google will choose not to take advantage, someday. Recently, Google has been opening up a discussion about how they make use of the information they gather, putting limits on how those data are used, and how long it is retained, as well as voluntarily forgoing some kinds of collection. Even if we trust Google implicitly with that data – and the company's recent efforts to be clearer about retention policies and to provide ways of limiting exposure are promising – it represents too valuable a target, some maintain, to be collected in one place.

Search, surveillance, and transparency

Science fiction author Cory Doctorow recently penned a short story (2007) that puts all of this into dystopic relief. In the story, a man returns to the United States after some time abroad, to find that the Department of Homeland Security has partnered with Google, and that they were using behavioral targeting to assess him as a risk. The story goes on to explain that, once on a watchlist, Google would allow the government to watch his every move. It appears to be the worst-case scenario of a distant future, but it is not. In 2005, a Canadian citizen was turned away at the Buffalo, New York, border crossing after border guards used Google to locate his blog and interrogate him about its contents (Vaas 2005). The same happened to a Canadian psychotherapist, whose identity as it appeared on Google included a description of drug use when he was younger (Solomon 2007). What makes Doctorow's story frightening is that the linchpin that would keep it from becoming a reality is very weak indeed. The two cases are, of course, different. Unlike Doctorow's story, US border patrol agents who turned away Canadian visitors made use of information freely available on the web, and more easily found using search engines. As Michael Zimmer (2008) has argued, the rise of a more sociable web ("Web 2.0") has created new sources of rich data about how people live their everyday lives, and, as a result, the kinds of things the border patrol, advertisers, and employers have access to is expanding rapidly. The problem in this case is really one of expectations. Since we expect our blog to be used only in particular contexts – and assessing our fitness to travel in a foreign country is not one of those contexts – the use of Google is surprising.

Several countries have used specialized search engines in order to locate illegal content within their own borders. An early Singaporean effort merely searched for files with image-related extensions, in order to find potential pornography (Ang & Nadarajan 1996). In 1999, the government-supported ISP SingNet faced popular dissent for "virus scanning" of computers on their network that led to the arrest of one network user when the search uncovered illegal materials. Although the World Wide Web represents a very large database to search, various forms of "policeware" – programs that allow for intrusion and the collection of large amounts of data – and signals intelligence programs also create huge databases that must be searched and sifted. Some of these closed databases are in private rather than public hands, and although search and data mining technologies are now being applied to them, they have existed in some form for as long as there have been national governments. But the public availability of fairly personal information is a newer phenomenon.

There are really two types of intrusions on our privacy. The first is the actual physical recording of an image or a piece of data. This extraction of information from our control need not be a serious breach. When we enter a convenience store, we do not generally glance at a security camera and assume that the images it is showing will show up on a video sharing site. At least, that is not what we expect today, although those expectations will be changing rapidly in the coming years. We are not particularly bothered by such intrusions because we trust, to some degree at least, that the images and data gathered will be handled appropriately – that the camera's tapes are not archived or shared, that our credit card number and shopping habits are not being sold to the highest bidder.

It is really that second step, the decontextualization of our information, that is particularly invasive. When the information that is collected by a security camera, or by a hotel's maid, or by a search engine is then used in a context that we did not expect or approve of, this can be disquieting. As a New Yorker, pizza makes up a substantial part of my diet, and the pizzeria down the block recognizes my voice, knows where I live, and knows how I like my "pie," as we say in these parts. I know that they know these things about me, and, far from bothering me, I enjoy the convenience of that trusted relationship. If, while traveling in London, I ordered room service only to find that the hotel knew what my favorite pizza toppings were, I would find this disturbing. It is true that it would still be an added value, but it would make me feel that I had less control over my environment than it had over me. Both my pizzeria and the hotel would have violated my confidence. It is all too easy for the personalization services of search engines to do the same thing: allow my relationship with the search engine to bleed over into my relationships with other companies and with the government. I do not want Google to know how I like my pie any more than I want the pizzeria to know how I like my search results.

The move toward more surveillance in society is not inevitable, and, likewise, there is no inherent necessity for search engines to collect and make use of information about us. There was a time when search engine developers paid very little attention to the transaction logs produced, and there is nothing that says that a return to that point is impossible. In practice, however, we enjoy the benefits that sharing this data provides. It is unlikely that many people will be willing to pick a less effective search engine just to avoid being profiled. It is important, therefore, that the degree to which we open our lives to search engines be proportionate to the degree to which search engines open up their own internal processes.

This extends equally to government surveillance. The idea that the police and intelligence communities should open their doors so that targets of their surveillance – the "bad guys" – can better understand the way they work is likely to be treated with more than a little suspicion. The police and intelligence communities have cultivated a culture of secrecy that has served them well in the past. Clearly, some sources of data cannot be openly accessible to the public. But there is value in knowing the kinds of data collected and the ways in which they are processed. Knowing more about how the government works allows us to balance the power of police authority with the need for public autonomy.

The global village and new legends

Wired Magazine at one point considered Marshall McLuhan to be its patron saint. His polysemous aphorisms appealed to the popular idea that technology changes everything. One of the memes that continues to survive is the idea of a "global village," and like so much of what McLuhan (1962) wrote, it is often interpreted quite differently by different people. The original conception saw a retribalization brought about by electronic mass media, and the potential for homogenization. The *digerati* appropriated the term, and suggested a global forum, a meeting of minds.

Early sociology drew heavily on Ferdinand Tönnies' (1957) distinction between people who are organized primarily as communities (*Gemeinschaft*), bound by familial and tribal expectations, and those who are organized as societies

(*Gesellschaft*), bound together by a shared goal. Simmel (1964) noted that the major difference between these groups was whether individuals could choose their own social ties. Particularly within cities, it was likely that a person would choose ties with others who might exist in completely separate communities. For example, I have social ties to many of my colleagues in the field of internet research (who also have ties to one another), and ties to members of my extended family (who also have ties to one another), as well as ties to people in my neighborhood, in previous neighborhoods, and in earlier workplaces. These connections are to groups that are not particularly connected. If I were to draw circles around the members of each of these groups, they would certainly intersect – since I am in each – but they would intersect very little. This differs from a traditional community, in which one might go to school with the same people one works with, one plays sports with, one vacations with, and one marries.

The internet is thought to encourage an even more extreme level of *Gesellschaft*, as we gain close relationships with those we might never meet in person (Walther 1996). Sherry Turkle (1996) has argued that this is the distinctive feature of identity online; just as we flip through applications on our computers, shifting our attention from context to context, we switch identities online to suit our needs. The reason for this is that our interactions, say, in a multi-user game can be easily walled off from our behavior in other social contexts online and off. But social technologies like blogs and social networking systems, along with search engines, make such walls very thin. The mark of *Gesellschaft* society is that we do not really know what our grown children are doing: they move off to a new city, and, except for the infrequent telephone call, they are strangers. Likewise, they know little of our private lives. A combination of social media and search engines changes that. There is a danger that search engines can conflate more than one person's life into the same impression of a person, but at the very least they draw together pieces of our lives that otherwise would not intersect. Students are surprised when they discover that recruiters are looking at pictures of them drunk and wild at a college party on Facebook. In some ways, though, this is a return to small-town life, where everyone knows everything about you. Under those constraints, it is more difficult to live a "double life."

As time goes on, we are witnessing a reversal of the nature of online networking, with those groups that were once segregated – family, friends, work, school – being integrated through the power of technologies that aggregate identifying information. The work of social media and search engines is being enhanced by community policies that insist on positively identifying members of the community as "real" individuals. Paypal, the online payment company, requires users to tie their account back to a bank account in order to root identities in the real world; Amazon attempts to certify real names for their reviews; and Second Life plans to do the same for the avatars in their communal virtual world. Several companies, including Aristotle and Trufina, as well as freely available software and protocols like OpenID, provide identity verification in some form for communities that want this. The idea is that trust is only possible when a real identity stands behind it.

There are ways to resist this. Readers of spy novels are familiar with the idea of a "legend," a cover story constructed to give the spy a believable background (Mahle 2006, p. 366). Those who spend a great deal of time online are probably equally aware of the usefulness of multiple identities. Sometimes, these are throwaway identities used to gain access to free resources that, nonetheless, require a user name. Gaining access to *Los Angeles Times* stories, for example, requires people to log in. Reluctant to share private information, many people simply invent a false login identity, or turn to a site like Bugmenot.com to use one of their proven identities. Sometimes people create false identities for fraudulent reasons: in order to steal money or services. Sometimes they create identities to do what they do not want to be associated with, "sockpuppets" that support them in public venues, or play the antagonist. Finally, many people keep a blog under the cover of a pseudonym in the hope that a search engine will not connect it with their "main" identity. Sometimes these identities are tied to a character played in a multiplayer online game.

At present, the only viable way of defending privacy while still maintaining a public life is the creation of masks and false identities. If the use of surveillance cameras in public spaces is any indication, it is likely that there will soon be both private rules against contributing pseudonymously to discussions, and possibly legal structures that restrict our ability to play a character rather than our "real" identity, where there are not already. It is important that we recognize that despite the dangers of allowing pseudonymous interactions, they are the best way of mitigating the loss of our personal privacy in a world where search engines peer into every part of our lives. As the integrating technologies of the search engine and social media bring down the walls between social contexts, people will take one of two paths: either give in to the integrating force, or for a few determined souls, develop far more intricate legends.

Many people are not alarmed by the idea that they might be observed by a machine. Few enter the local convenience store and feel oppressed by the eye of the camera above them. The collection of data does not seem intrusive until it is networked, findable, and available to a wide group of people. Search engines will provide the technology to aggregate each of these small intrusions into a wholesale removal of distance between our public and private lives. It seems unlikely that this will change. The most promising solution is perhaps counterintuitive: we must increase the transparency of the search engine.

While the technologies of surveillance continue to expand, those same technologies can be employed to reduce the secrecy of corporations and governments as well as individuals. Many individuals have chosen an exhibitionist path, blogging their everyday interactions, hopes, and dreams. But in exchange for this disclosure, they expect organizations to reciprocate. If they watch us, we should be able to watch them. Mann, Nolan, and Wellman (2003) term this "sousveillance," watching from below, and see it as a way of confronting organizations by using their tools against them. Their work is grounded in the assumption that surveillance is a technology of social power, and that by confronting those who are engaging in surveillance with an inversion of the technology, an opportunity for discussion is presented.

An alternative approach suggests not so much "watching from below" as "watching from beside." Observation is not the problem; the problem is an unequal distribution of the observing and the observed. As Amitai Etzioni (1999) argues, the right kinds of transparency reduce, rather than increase, the necessity for government control and intrusion, and scrutiny is the antidote to control. Many take issue with Etzioni's communitarian approach to privacy and transparency, the idea that, in a global village, the villagers should be watching one another.[4] The putative needs for camera surveillance in a shop – to stop shoplifting and prevent criminal acts in the store – are better met by a culture of mutual respect, along with peer-to-peer reciprocal observation. The degree to which search engines allow us to watch each other, and to watch the search engine, will determine the degree to which it is performing as an ethical member of the global community. David Brin (1998) suggests that this kind of reciprocal transparency is our last, best chance of creating an open and creative society. He acknowledges that there are dangers – for example, that we will become obsessed with each other's lives in the same way we seem to be obsessed with celebrities today – and it is clear that this alone will do little more than partially mitigate the present imbalances, but it is worth taking those risks if there is the potential it will lead to a sustained open society.

At present, it is impossible for us to know who sees the information search engines collect and under what conditions that occurs. In 2002, a cartoon appeared in the *New Yorker* in which a person tells his friend "I can't explain it – it's just a funny feeling that I'm being Googled." If only we had a kind of search engine radar that told us who was looking for information about us and why; the equivalent of the red light on a camera that lets us know we are being recorded. More than just a dot on a screen, this would inform us of when, for example, Google was combining data from Google Mail with our search histories or medical histories.[5] The first rule for search engines when it comes to privacy and transparency should be: take only what you are willing to give. The clickstreams and other data generated by individuals using the web are valuable, and when the trade is transparent, many people will be willing to exchange it for services. But when search engines collect data without clearly explaining how they will make use of it, and to whom they will release it, it represents an unjust imbalance of power.

CHAPTER SEVEN

Sociable Search

The term "social search" is redundant, but that has not reduced its recent popularity. The technological practices that allow for a search engine to exist depend on social interactions. Search engines rely on the social behaviors of their users, the socially defined structure of the World Wide Web, and our collective creation of knowledge in order to meet other social needs. The idea that search could be anything but social is absurd. Nonetheless, in recent years the term "social search" has appeared more widely, referring to technologies that draw explicitly on connections among people in order to find information more effectively.

If search engines have always been social, they are now becoming more *sociable*. While "social" and "sociable" share the same Latin root, meaning "to unite," the latter connotes a certain degree of companionship, a friendly form of interaction. Judith Donath (2004) has pioneered the use of the term "sociable media," which she defines as those media that "enhance communication and the formation of social ties among people." She distinguishes this approach from ideas that focus on information retrieval. Rather than increasing the flow or accumulation of information, sociable systems perform best when they fulfill the social needs of the community, allowing for the appropriate distribution of attention and social interaction. There already exists a literature surrounding "social navigation" (Munro, Höök, & Benyon 1999; Svensonn et al. 2001), but "sociable search" goes beyond systems designed to help groups make sense of an information source, and toward building social capital within search communities.

As with many functions now performed automatically, the process of indexing the web was initially performed by individuals exercising their own judgment. It takes only a glance behind the curtain to recognize that current search engines, while their processes may be automated, still perform in large part through the collection of latent human judgment applied to the content of the web and the value of particular pages. Most search engines now rely implicitly on the links drawn from blogs and other websites, just as web surfers explicitly follow those links. But there has been a revival of openly engaging human judgment in the process of web search. Blogging has spawned a host of social software that is designed to help to connect people together, and those connections mean new ways of finding experts and locating expertise.

As many people look to the future of search, their focus falls on social networks and information sharing. This idea of the social nature of navigation can be traced back to the "trails" of hyperlinks Vannevar Bush (1945) suggested more than sixty years ago, but there remains the pressing question of how best to harness that social component. In this chapter, we will begin by examining collaborative filtering systems: distributed approaches to discovering what information is collectively regarded as most interesting. We will then look to the question of the relationship of experts to expertise; sometimes the information we need remains in someone's head, and we need a way of locating that tacit knowledge. One particular area in which this becomes important is the functioning of informed democratic processes: public engagement in policy and political campaigns. Sociable search has already gained a foothold in this venue.

As the Rolling Stones remind us, there is always a tension between finding what you want, and getting what you need. The emergence of sociable search suggests that we need to find not just information, but each other. Search is important for the individual who wants to be part of a larger social conversation and provides a tool for gaining social efficacy, but a tool capable of linking people together to build social capital and develop collective intelligence is even more important. Searching and browsing represent closely tied forms of finding information online, and sociable search seeks to combine them to discover new ways of navigating our online worlds.

Collaborative filtering

The division between taxonomies, like those offered early on by Yahoo and the Open Directory Project, and search engines is not as clear as it might at first appear. Both approaches are used in order to find and navigate to a page that, the user hopes, will lead to some information that will help to fulfill the goal of the search. Many early search engines combined the two approaches, and search has often been not of the entire web, but instead of a human-created taxonomy. When Yahoo's taxonomy grew too large and complex to quickly browse, for example, it provided a search function for that content. Even the most automated search systems have relied on human coding to some extent.

As we have seen, search engines often draw on tacit interactions – the structure of the web, searchers' clicks through results pages, and the like – to improve their search capability. There are groups of alternative systems that instead draw on explicit reviews and coding by large groups of site members. This kind of distribution of a large project has been deemed "crowdsourcing" (J. Howe 2006), a play on the word "outsourcing" that refers to online structures that promote mass collaboration. Not all tasks are amenable to this kind of distribution; many kinds of tasks do not continue to benefit from each new person added to the team working on the problem. For some projects, more people can actually increase the amount of time it takes to complete the task (Brooks 1995). But search is the classic task that benefits equally from each new person added to the problem. Distributed approaches to computing have found their greatest application in the search for extraterrestrials and in analyzing permutations of protein folding (SETI@Home and folding@home, respectively). Just as those projects leverage small amounts of computing power from a large number of machines to search problem spaces, sociable search systems provide an infrastructure for aggregating the small judgments of a large number of individuals.

This form of structured, distributed browsing tends to be especially good at discovering new sites that meet a general user need. As we have seen, search engines are meant to be as flexible as possible, but often assume that a person has a fairly clear search goal in mind: something like "I want to find the most likely cause of a rash on my arm." In practice, many people turn to the web to find out "What are some amusing images of cats that I have not yet seen?" or "What is something on the web that can entertain me?" or, more generally still, "What news items are interesting to people like me?"

Collaborative filtering sites are designed to provide answers to the questions above in a way that requires little action on the part of the user. We could look at a number of levels of such personalization. At a very basic level, a person chooses the newspaper that best suits them, or turns to a television channel, even without knowing the content, because they suspect that The Cartoon Network or Cable News Network will present them with content that they will be interested in. Personalization often refers to a step beyond the choice of channel. Work in the early 1980s at the Massachusetts Institute of Technology aimed to create a *Daily Me*, a newspaper that reflected the specific interests of each reader (Brand 1987). Generally, these systems discovered readers' interests by asking them to identify a set of topics. This process, as one of these researchers has more recently noted, is in many ways analogous to a search engine query (Bender 2002). Both represent a kind of editorial function, creating a "front page" of stories from a world of possibilities, based on explicit criteria provided by the user.

This sort of explicit filtering is fine, but assumes that users are willing to indicate their preferences, and that they actually know their preferences, neither of which is necessarily true. Collaborative filtering allows for those who share similar interests to collaborate to discover relevant materials, with very little individual effort. Some of the first successful online collaborative filters were designed to filter out comments in a discussion that were not particularly interesting. Slashdot represents a blog that has for some time provided, as their motto makes clear, "News for Nerds. Stuff that matters." The process by which that news was gathered differed very little from the filtering process at, for example, a daily newspaper. A small number of editors examined news submitted by the readership and others, and decided which items should receive a short abstract and be placed on the front page. These articles often received hundreds of comments within a short space of time. Some of these comments were well informed, or at least amusing, but were buried by hundreds of non-relevant, erroneous, or redundant comments. Rather than editing the comments, the creators of Slashdot left this up to randomly selected visitors to the site, who were asked to rate some of the comments, either increasing or decreasing each comment's overall score by one. This collaborative method allowed readers to look at only the best comments, by viewing only those that were above some selected threshold, and to ignore the large number of less worthy comments. This process, while it clearly established authorities, seemingly did so without reference to the traditional markers of authority that tend to hold sway in other contexts (Poor 2005).

Slashdot, like a number of influential blogs, has the ability to uncover websites that would otherwise have remained an obscure part of the millions of rarely visited sites, and quickly direct a flood of traffic to them. Search engines can also shape traffic, of course, and attracting attention from search engines remains a task many webmasters strive for. But filter sites like Slashdot can open up a flood of traffic in a very short period of time. This led to something users called the "Slashdot Effect." Small websites quickly became overwhelmed by the flash crowds caused by a link on a major filter site, and often shut down under the duress (Adler 1999). This continues to occur with many of the major filter sites, including Fark and Digg. Arriving on a search engine results page is important to those who create content for the web, since it assures that visitors will discover their page, but given that collaborative filters provide the equivalent of one results page for all of their users, appearing on the front page of a major filter site can represent a massive change in the collective attention, bringing a once obscure webpage quickly to the fore.

Digg represents a new generation of such filters because it shares the same collaborative filtering of comments, but has extended this to the selection of stories as well. Unlike Slashdot, which has traditionally relied on editors to make up the front page, Digg turned this function over to the collective will of its members (filtered through a somewhat obscure algorithm) from the outset. Because Digg has a large number of users, its front page represents a kind of generalized answer to the search query "What is interesting today?" Users can also examine who else is likely to "Digg" (vote as noteworthy) pages they are interested in, and can fine-tune the answer to that general question by recognizing who shares their particular interests.

All of this works under the assumption that preferences in one area are likely to translate to tastes across topics. This is generally the case. Sociologists have long noted that homophily, the tendency of like-minded people to "flock together," tends to be self-reinforcing (McPherson, Smith-Lovin, & Cook 2001). If two people have similar backgrounds and preferences on a range of matters, they are likely to have similar tastes in other areas, leading to even greater congruence. We have already encountered Pierre Bourdieu's views on the role of taste in the structuring and restructuring of society. Collaborative filters like Digg represent an interesting example of a kind of agonistic field that does away with many of the obvious markers that allow for distinctions of taste, and is reduced mainly to the explicit ranking of various choices. By reducing some of the cues that might otherwise interfere with collaborative work, as well as the transaction costs normally entailed in such collaboration, these systems represent an opportunity to incorporate a more diverse and resilient group of searchers, even within topically or interest-constrained collections of users (Chi & Pirolli 2006). It is too soon to know how exactly affiliations created via social filters – "implicit cultures" as they have been termed (Blanzieri & Giorgini 2000) – affect other areas of social experience, though their use in the political sphere suggests changes in a number of institutions are likely.

There are several of these kinds of filters, in addition to Digg, often with slightly different operating processes, addressing different aims, and catering to different languages and cultures. StumbleUpon, Reddit, i-am-bored, and netvibes, for example, may appear to have slightly different functions, but serve the same ultimate role: concentrating attention on sites that have been identified collaboratively. Likewise, their initial intents may have been different, but in practice bookmarking and tagging sites like del.icio.us, Furl, CiteULike, and even the tag-centric pages of Technorati have come to do much the same thing: allow individuals to locate sites they did not know they were looking for. All of these represent either an alternative to the search engine or an opportunity to make search work better (Yanbe et al. 2007).

The bottom-up categorization of websites, resulting in what has come to be called "folksonomies," represents an alternative to the top-down organization (even when collaboratively created) of taxonomies (Vander Wal 2005). The individual web surfer may have no intention of creating an overarching organizational structure, but in attaching idiosyncratic tags to a given bookmark, she is helping to associate it with other pages, and associate herself with other surfers. This process, when taken collectively, results in what Weinberger (2007) refers to as the "externalization of meaning," a way of attaching metadata as commentary and connecting ideas explicitly. By the end of 2006, more than a quarter of US internet users were tagging the content of the web, and that number is expected to continue to grow (Rainie 2007). Bookmarking is essentially a search technology, a way of re-finding information. By opening those bookmarks to others, bookmarking systems recapitulate the phylogeny of web search. One of the earliest methods of finding one's way around the web was to rely on someone's published list of bookmarks. By allowing users to see one another's trails of bookmarks, we are engaged in a never-ending process of social remembering.

There has been some discussion regarding whether these new forms of social search are preparing to unseat the major search engines, and particularly the Google juggernaut. At first, this seems to be a comparison of two very dissimilar kinds of services. Search engines are designed as indexes, allowing for particular terms to be located anywhere on the web. "Sociable search" instead acts to aggregate evaluations of content, or collect sites that are favored by communities. While this may describe their operation in the purest form, in reality they lean much closer to one another. Both sociable search and traditional search engines browse the web seeking appropriate pages to index, but search that is enabled by social networking seems to uncover relevant pages that general-purpose search engines leave behind. Search engines, recognizing that indexing alone is not enough, also attempt to measure the community's evaluation of a site, inferring that information from link structures and other facets of the site, but again, by explicitly taking into account the searchers' social networks, results are even more effectively ranked (Mislove, Gummadi, & Druschel 2006). Both sociable search and traditional search require the generation of summaries of the pages, though it seems again that sociable search may have an edge here (Boydell & Smyth 2007). Like most large sites, bookmarking sites and collaborative filters generally provide the ability to search their contents in a more traditional way, and, more and more frequently, pages from the major social filter sites like Digg are showing up in search engine results pages of Google and other general-purpose search engines. In practice, both perform the same function – concentrating public attention – either by rating indexes of the web, or by indexing ratings of the web.

Digg and similar websites may not be actively seeking community as their goal, just as social bookmarking sites like del.icio.us do not have that intent. But by making the actions of their users transparent to a certain degree, they provide the opportunity for sociability and the creation of social capital. Erickson and Kellogg (2000) have described this property as "social translucence," a certain degree of visibility among those who are using a resource. Being aware of other users of a system allows for better coordination of effort, and increased trust. Search engines trade on the ideal of trust; we need to know that they are neither unintentionally nor intentionally aiming to mislead. But the indirect observation of self-interested and cooperative users of collaborative filtering and bookmarking sites provides a basis for building trust that traditional search engines will find difficult to match.

What seems more likely is that the use of collaborative filtering will become integrated within a larger ecology of findability. At present, only the most experienced users of the web are participating in these collaborative systems. Over time, a larger proportion of users are likely to be collaboratively filtering, but this will not eliminate the need for more proactive searching to fulfill specified needs. Much of what occurs on these systems is perhaps better considered as social browsing, while social search makes use of social relationships to augment traditional searching processes (Freyne et al. 2007). Elements of sociable search already exist in many search engines, and it appears that there continues to be an ongoing convergence toward these types of systems.

Bringing humans back

Social connections are already central to most search engines, if only implicitly. The PageRank system, for example, infers the quality of a site based on social judgments. It never asks humans directly which pages are most authoritative, but, as Jon Kleinberg (1999) notes, hyperlinks "encode a considerable amount of latent human judgments," and researchers have long noted the similarity between social networks and hypertext (Kumar et al. 2002). While collaborative filters and other forms of sociable search may rely to some degree on latent judgments, they are usually fairly overt in how opinions are recorded. Recently, traditional search engines have attempted to actively incorporate the social element into their systems.

The two most anticipated search engines of 2007 were Mahalo and Wikia Search, which shared more than a penchant for unusual names. Just as search engines once enhanced the usefulness of directories crafted by hand, that kind of human expertise is finding its way back into search. However, the ways in which those humans are employed differs significantly from search engine to search engine. Mahalo (with the tag-line "human-centered search"), rather than relying on massive automatic crawling of the web, provides search results pages that are written by editors, much in the same way that About.com, Answers.com, and Wikipedia provide topical information. This might seem to be a Sisyphean task, particularly given the speed at which the internet is expanding, and creating and maintaining an extremely large number of search results pages is a significant challenge, but by focusing on the most general searches and providing results that are tuned to such broad needs, there is the potential for providing for a particular kind of topical search that the general-purpose indexes are ill equipped to handle.

Wikia Search is an effort led by someone who has experience with the epitome of crowdsourced online resources: Wikipedia pioneer Jimmy Wales (Deutschman 2007). Launching at the beginning of 2008, at the time of writing it is only in the earliest stages of development, but some of the excitement surrounding the project owes much to the success of Wikipedia, and the feeling that, if there is an alternative paradigm for navigating the web, it will probably contain some component of mass collaboration and crowdsourcing. Wikia Search incorporates many of the recommendations of inclusion and transparency recommended above. Not only does it build in transparency in the ranking algorithms, it plans to make each of the pieces that make up the engine available to others to build their own search engines. Over the next several years, we are likely to encounter a number of alternatives that combine traditional indexing search engines with a variety of human-coded content, whether that is accumulated through semantic markup, tagging, or some other mechanism.

Other search engines are attempting to incorporate social filtering in various small ways, making the common kinds of implicit metrics of popularity more explicit. Aftervote (www.aftervote.com) seeks to combine many of the features found on search engines in the past (indeed, it is a metasearch engine, and does not do its own crawling), and make them available to users who are seeking more control. One of those features is the ability to explicitly vote on the relevancy of results, collectively reordering the results pages. Even when search engines are not choosing to integrate social systems, users are doing it for them. A plug-in for the Firefox browser, for example, integrates StumbleUpon ratings into the Google search results pages. Those pages that have been reviewed by members of StumbleUpon have a bit of green-colored text next to the titles, providing a category and rating that have been assigned by other StumbleUpon users.

The question of whether these new, more "human" approaches to search will work is less related to the technological questions than it is to the social questions. Will the engines be able to attract enough knowledge work, on a great enough scale, to lead people away from the comfort of a familiar search box? Each of these approaches requires an investment of human cognition. Google has taken to heart the advice Steve Krug gives to interface designers: "Don't make me think" (Krug 2006). Google's greatest virtue is that it is able to provide a single-stop search engine with results pages that behave in predictable ways. Nonetheless, not all search is the same, and each of these new efforts represents a way of drawing in collective human organization to assist in making the online world more navigable.

Social networks and search for expertise

This spectrum of collaborative filtering extends beyond finding information, and bleeds into finding information for people, about people, and ultimately connecting with those people. The site del.icio.us allows individuals to use an explicit tag to indicate that something might be interesting "for" someone else (e.g. "for: alex_halavais"), making it a kind of link messaging service. Major social networking systems, sites like Facebook or LinkedIn, allow people to search for user-supplied profiles and connect to others in the network. And many of these systems provide various ways of tapping into the individual knowledge and abilities of others on the network, by prompting users to make explicit affiliations, by inferring relationships between people, and by providing an easy route to their expertise.

Some collaborative filters are designed to support social ties outside of the internet and in the physical world. Upcoming.com provides information about events that are happening, mostly, in physical spaces. Users of the system are able to indicate whether or not they plan to attend any given event, and provide an attendees' social calendar of sorts. Of course, if two people seem to be attending many of the same events, they might conclude they have something in common and meet up. Those kinds of interest-based ties are the goal of a site like Meetup, of course, and a number of other dating social networking systems.

Again, the idea that social networking systems are in some way related to search may seem odd at first blush, but, as we have seen above, search has always been tied to social networks. Collaborative filtering and bookmarking systems provide some degree of social translucence, allowing for the effects of social networks to be more clearly recognized. At the same time, social networking systems like Facebook often seem to lack a *raison d'être*; once someone has identified their friends, it is not immediately obvious how that network might be employed. One of the most natural ways of making use of that network is to find information. As we have seen, there is a good chance that someone affiliated with you is more likely to be able to provide relevant referrals. By mining our social networks, we provide some basis for finding and evaluating resources on the web (Kautz, Selman, & Shah 1997).

Social networking systems also tend to promote the kind of social information seeking we do every day. For many types of problems, we are seeking the human repository of expertise and knowledge. Why would we become an expert on a topic if it is possible to find an existing expert? There has been quite a bit of research questioning how we find people who are likely to know something, and how this extends to electronic networks (Adamic & Adar 2005). The task of searching a social network is structurally similar to searching the web at large. People are in some ways like webpages: they hold information, they are connected in various ways, and those connections lend them a certain degree of prestige or authority. Understanding how we search our social networks, then, gives us some indication of how we might search the web at large. But understanding how we search our social networks in other contexts can also help us to search our social networks online (J. Zhang & Ackerman 2005). Indeed, searching our social network for experts before we search the rest of the web can often help us to reach our goal more quickly, and create a community of searchers (Ribak, Jacovi, & Soroka 2002).

The search capability of many social networking systems is really two sides of the same coin: finding information about people you know, and finding people based on certain characteristics. First, social networking systems often provide an environment for searching for information about people. The names of some of the more popular dating sites – Match.com, Friendfinder, MatchMaker – hint at this search function. Of course, there are a number of new vertical search engines that focus on finding information about people, but the social networking and dating sites have provided such a function for some time. Typing someone's name into a general-purpose search engine is unlikely to yield biographical information or a résumé. That biographical information is more likely to be found on LinkedIn, Match.com, or on Monster.com. As noted earlier, these represent a sort of replacement for the Farley File or Rolodex of the past, and there is some evidence that this is the more common use of systems like Facebook, rather than to locate people that are unknown to the searcher (Lampe, Ellison, & Steinfield 2006).

These services also provide an important complementary function: the ability to search by characteristic and find a group of people who match a particular search query. There were certainly pre-internet analogues for such reverse searches – as in, for example, of criminal records indexed by criminal history and *modi operandi* that could yield a pool of suspects – but the ability to do this more easily and for a broader number of people has far-reaching effects. Searches in this context are often narrowly tailored. A user might want to index any mention of "cats" against dating profiles, replicating a traditional indexed search by term, but often searches of profiles consist of characteristics that are measured along an established set of scales, from age, to religion, to physical appearance. In the case of employment databases – both those operated by large corporations, and public sites like Monster.com – the characteristics of greatest interest are often the skills, knowledge, and experience of the people who are indexed. As more business is conducted in ad hoc groups and networks, searching for appropriate expertise becomes more frequent, and more important. Finding the right expert within the organization or outside of it is a way of finding a "site" of information. That process can be helped by systems that allow for people search, and social networking systems are a natural place for this to occur (Becerra-Fernandez 2006).

We have already seen that search engines have difficulty with the "deep web," but the deepest part of this is what we might call the "wet web": the information that remains stuck in people's brains, the tacit knowledge that has not been recorded in indexed form. A good search can uncover a great deal of information, but knowledge and wisdom are notoriously difficult to separate from their human hosts. Given this, a complete search should yield not only text, images, video, and other forms of information, but people with particular expertise.

The most obvious way of doing this is by creating a market for answering questions, and several such markets exist. Yahoo, Live, Amazon, and LinkedIn each provide a question-and-answer system, as do a number of stand-alone sites like Wondir. Generally, these sites allow individuals to ask a question and then for either the information-seekers or any participant to rate the various answers. In some cases, this is all that is provided, while in others, points are awarded, and the market is largely reputation-based. For a time Google provided a paid answers exchange, as have others. All of these systems attempt to gain expert opinion without the unneeded overhead of locating and hiring an expert. Outside consultants can be expensive not only because their expertise comes at a premium, but because of the expense of finding and interacting with them. For a single question, that expense is frequently overwhelming. By providing the infrastructure for asking questions and having them answered, such systems remove some of the organizational barriers to reaching the knowledge in other people's heads.

In many cases, the questions asked are not particularly esoteric, and might be found in some form on the internet. Popular questions on the Yahoo Answers site, for example, include those about traveling on airplanes with infants and the title of a half-remembered book. This is information that is already out on the web and indexed, but requires human help to determine what is credible, filter out the less important elements, and synthesize it into a concise whole. LinkedIn and Facebook (by way of a third-party plug-in) both provide question-answering abilities, with the added benefit of being able to easily ascertain the background and experience of the person answering.

In some aspects, this echoes other ways in which the web is being used to commodify and trade the labor of knowledge workers. Several websites provide services to locate and hire outsourced technical labor. By acting as a kind of global eBay of labor, even for relatively small projects, this provides new ways of generating value and selling it on a relatively open market. This commodification of expertise is happening at precisely the same time as many people are gifting their intellectual labor, on small and large scales, to collaborative projects with a public benefit. Wikipedia continues to stand as an example of something created by the accumulation of millions of man-hours of donated expertise and expression, and the blogosphere, though less centralized, provides another example.

This all suggests changes in the way that society creates, shares, and evaluates knowledge. To what degree is "truth" determined by findability and the endorsement of peers? Other trends in social computing, particularly those focusing on user-created content, are driven in part by our focus on search engines as a means for discovering materials, rather than relying on traditional institutional sources of authority. What does this new form of authority mean for the process of thinking collectively, and for our ideas of how to evaluate the credibility of sources?

(Re)Finding community

All of this suggests a move from goal-oriented searching for information, to a desire to build both explicit and tacit connections between people. The idea that either are possible in an online world is ridiculed by some. After all, an individual sitting in front of a computer screen certainly appears to be about as anti-social as possible. Moreover, the kinds of social interaction that person engages in online seem to lack both fidelity and depth. Relationships of trust and reputation are simulated in the online world, represented and quantified as a score, and available to all.

The eBay rating is the perfect example of this. Why should you trust someone on eBay enough to send them money? You have no reason to believe that they are human, let alone trustworthy. However, a number next to their name indicates the track record of this user within the marketplace, and by clicking this you can discover how others have ranked the person. Despite not knowing anyone, you have some level of automatic trust that allows for a financial transaction to take place. This in some ways represents the apex of capitalism: buyer and seller in a frictionless environment of exchange, with attention and reputation reduced to scores.

In an earlier chapter, your focus was drawn to the idea of an attention economy. The new social locations on the web create economies of reputation as well. Cory Doctorow has also written about such economies. In his novelette *Down and Out in the Magic Kingdom* (2003), characters live in a world in which the money economy has disappeared, replaced by "whuffie," easily exchangeable goods and services. In reality, there is not yet a single currency for reputation, and it is sometimes difficult to differentiate attention from reputation. If someone is listed as a friend by 1,200 Facebook members, does this mean they have a particularly strong reputation or that they manage to draw attention to themselves? Does that distinction really matter, when either has been commoditized and is tradable, and the mere ability to measure the degree of connectedness makes it worthy of pursuit – the ultimate portable wealth in an era of "liquid modernity" (Bauman 2000, pp. 153–4). Of course, much is missing in this one-dimensional trading floor, but the ability to create a more perfect, flexible market of exchange is gained.

It would be fair to assume that such explicit trust networks crowd out what – perhaps confusingly – has come to be called "social capital." In 1997, Langdon Winner decried the loss of small community bookstores in the face of online retailers like Amazon.com, noting that bookstores were more than merely a place to buy books, they were a place to meet and talk about ideas. Pierre Bourdieu has defined social capital as "the aggregate of the actual or potential resources which are linked to possession of a durable network of more or less institutionalized relationships of mutual acquaintance and recognition" (1986, p. 248). That is a very broad definition, and the term has been interpreted in a dizzying number of ways, many of them at odds with one another (Foley & Edwards 1999). Many share the idea that mass society and mass culture atomizes the individual, and under these conditions it is unlikely that she will protect and nurture the institutions of democracy. The challenge was to find ways of maintaining and building sociability, or, in William Kornhauser's words, "if men are to remain civilized or become so, the art of associating together must grow and improve in the same ratio in which the equality of conditions is increased" (1960, p. 32). Amazon.com has gradually introduced social interaction of various sorts on their site, though it may remain a pale shadow of what was available in a small local bookshop. By creating structures that both exploit and build the connections between individuals, there is a potential not only to allow citizens to find information – a vital ingredient of good government – but also to build the informal institutions that ensure the continuation of that government.

The goal-oriented exchange behaviors of the marketplace can lead to abbreviated social links, but it is not necessarily the case that these quantified relationships replace deeper civic engagement. Some have argued that new technologies have replaced the traditional organizations of civil society. This case has been made, perhaps, most famously by Robert Putnam, who has argued that the decline in groups like bowling leagues in the United States are emblematic of the replacement of our more sociable leisure-time activities with more individualized pursuits like watching television (1995). There is something puzzling in the idea that bowling can support the development of strong civil society, but – as in the case of Digg – the process of collaboratively working through news and events to uncover the most interesting is seen as antithetical to the same kind of development of strong ties.

In both cases, the idea is that sociability leads to conversation, conversation to deliberation, and deliberation to some form of political consensus and action. Michael Schudson (1997) suggests that the idea that conversation alone is the germ of democratic participation is probably too simple; conversation is hardly unique to democratic societies. He argues that democratically oriented conversation is "not essentially spontaneous but essentially rule-governed, essentially *civil*, and unlike the kinds of conversation often held in highest esteem for their freedom and their wit, it is essentially oriented to *problem-solving*." Not all conversations that occur online, from distributed blog conversations to the chatter on YouTube, would rise to this level. But cooperating to build an understanding, in working together toward collective knowledge, provides the grounds for forming tacit connections and the skills necessary to work collaboratively toward problem-solving.

Search 2.0

Pundits have labeled the wide range of new social applications of the internet "Web 2.0," suggesting that it represents an evolution of web technologies. The above has focused on several sites that engage in some form of collaboration in order to make sense of the online world. We could easily add others to the mix. Wikipedia has been frequently credited as an open, collaborative alternative to keyword-based search, for example. More important than any given website, though, is the idea of sociable search, an idea that is making its way into every sort of site on the web. When you see the term "folksonomy" used, del.icio.us and Flickr are held up as exemplars, but the idea of tagging increasingly shows up in a very wide range of websites. Web feeds (RSS) were once associated mainly with blogs, but now appear in a very broad range of contexts. The "site" for observing sociable search is not a single website, but the information ecology at large.

Rather than a site or an army of sites rising up to challenge Google, Yahoo, Ask.com, and the others, sociable search represents a way of making things more findable from the outset, and a way of thinking about the process of search in terms of more than simply a "search results page." It would be presumptuous to label it a movement, and inaccurate since it is strikingly unaware of itself. Instead, sociable search is at the heart of the creation of a new kind of collective intelligence. Pierre Lévy (1997) writes that the new knowledge environment leads to "a re-creation of the social bond based on reciprocal apprenticeship, shared skills, imagination, and collective intelligence . . . Intelligence must be understood here in its etymological sense of joining together (*inter legere*), as uniting not only ideas but people" (p. 10). At least at this point in their evolution, search engines do very little to bring people together. Those that fail to become sociable will be abandoned for different options that are more responsive to our personal and social knowledge needs.

The term "search party" has been used in the English language for hundreds of years, a linguistic reminder of the communal nature of search. Perhaps it is appropriate to think of sociable search as a kind of search party as well: a convivial effort to discover new ideas, entertainment, and knowledge together; a coming together that results in new, shared knowledge, as well as new social structures that may improve future searches. Search has always implicitly relied on social creation and assessment of knowledge. For search to serve the needs of society, it must not only connect people to information, but also connect people to each other. Search engines provide not only a gateway to knowledge for the individual, but an engine for change in social organization and collective patterns of knowledge-making.

CHAPTER EIGHT

Future Finding

At present, we think of search engines largely as a way to find information. In practice, we are already using them to find people and places as well. As we move to what has been termed an "internet of things," we begin to move beyond an index of knowledge, and toward an index of everything. As the sociable web grows to include not only the services we are familiar with, but collaborative virtual and augmented realities, the central position of search engines in social life will continue to gain strength.

What does that future search engine look like? There are indications both of technological alternatives to the current state of search, and of organizational differences. Experimental search engines present information in a map of clustered topics, or collect information from our life and use it to infer search restrictions. Just as the creation of content has been distributed in interesting ways over the last few years, there are indications that a centralized search engine may be just one of a number of alternatives for those engaging the social world online.

A 14-year-old subject in a study by Lewis and Fabos (2005) suggested "Everybody does it. I've grown up on it. It's like how you felt about stuff when you were growing up." She was talking about instant messaging, but the same could easily be said of search engines. They now feed into the background of our everyday activities and media use, only of note when they are frustratingly absent. Search engines remain in the news because of the clashes between the search giants and traditional sources of institutional power. While this has held our attention, research into new ways of wrangling the web continues. What does the future of search hold?

In the near term, many wonder what technologies might, as one commentator suggested, dethrone Google as the "start page of the internet" (Sterling 2007). This final chapter briefly explores some common predictions about the direction of search, and what these changes might mean for our social lives in the next decade.

Everything findable

Eric Brewer (2001) dreams of a search engine that will let him find things in his chaotic office. Because we have learned to turn to search, it can be frustrating when something is not searchable, but every day more of the world is becoming searchable.

The first step of this is to make all text searchable. The computer brought about two surprises. First, productivity did not increase, it decreased, and documents took more work to prepare instead of less. Second, the paperless office never really happened, and paper use has increased rather than decreased. Gradually, however, things are being born digital and never make their way onto paper. People bank, file their taxes, hand in their homework, distribute memos, and publish books online. All this digital media becomes fodder for search engines. While it may not yet be part of the general-purpose search engines like Google or Yahoo, eventually the contents of all of these work flows are likely to show up there as well, at least for those who are permitted to access them. There are even services that will open your mail and scan it for you, so that paper never pollutes your office. Optical character recognition (OCR) technologies are improving to such a degree that they are increasingly able to recognize written texts, as well as printed texts, allowing for at least partial indexing of hand-written documents for access in search engines (Milewski 2006). Under those conditions, Brewer's searchable office is almost here.

Things that were recorded in books, on audio tape, and on film are gradually being digitized, and often opened up to the web. Major book scanning projects by Google, Amazon, and the Internet Archive (supported by Microsoft and Yahoo) are aiming to unlock hundreds of years of printing and make it searchable. Once images, audio, and video are scanned, the question is how they will be made searchable. Especially now that do-it-yourself video is so common on the web, finding a way of searching that material – short of relying on creators and commentators to describe it in some useful way – has proven difficult. A great deal of current research is dedicated to extracting meaningful features from video, identifying faces, and recognizing music and speech.

A number of companies are working at making sense of the continual streams of data that are available. BBN Technologies, for example, has created a Broadcast Monitoring System, which detects speech and translates it in real time. It makes it possible to search for terms in your own language and find whether they have been mentioned in a broadcast anywhere in the world.

Some of the greatest innovations over the last few years have been in moving the once arcane field of geographical information systems into the public eye. Not only is there the possibility of using a searcher's geographical context to find "what's near me," but mapping and visualization products allow for far easier searching for locations, and navigating to those locations. Mapping will continue to improve with higher resolution and more quickly updated views. Google's Street View makes navigating through cities far easier, and no doubt this will continue to expand. By identifying the times and places videos and photographs were taken, it is possible to compile a profile of a location, assembled through a number of disparate records. Experimental robotic airships designed to deliver city-wide wireless connections also promise real-time aerial views of a city, a staple of science fiction (Haines 2005; Williams 2005). Google's investment in 23andme, a site that provides information about subscribers' DNA, hints at another staple of science fiction (Herper 2007).

The move into the real world, facilitated by RFID tags, GPS devices, and locative technologies leads us toward a "web of things," in which we grow even closer to Brewer's ideal. When every object you own is locatable by a radio beacon, Google will be able to find your keys (under the sofa), your favorite novel (at your friend's house), and your spouse (at the pub). Do you want your search for kiwi yoghurt to be global, limited to your own refrigerator, or limited to any of the refrigerators in the building? The primary use of RFID-tagged objects will be to interact with the environment and with specialized systems, but given that search was about real-world objects way before it was about electronic documents on a worldwide network, we can expect that our physical environments will eventually become searchable.

We begin to get a view of this universal search in the multi-user virtual environment Second Life. Each object in the world, from trees to turtles to toupées, has an associated object identifier. Many of the searches in Second Life feel very similar to their "real life" analogs: looking for the closest bank, finding people interested in backgammon, or looking for the best shop for discount shoes, for example. But because every object in the world is searchable, it creates new challenges for the infrastructure of search. Here, a crawler must actually move through the space, cataloging objects that may move the moment that crawler leaves the room. These objects may be bought or sold, combined or reassembled, duplicated or completely destroyed. Especially as individuals gain greater access to personal fabricators (see Gershenfeld 2005), devices capable of "printing" an object designed on a computer, these issues will begin to be translated into the real world as well. As search engines are called on to index more than just "documents," new challenges will certainly arise.

Memory prosthetics

In the film *Strange Days* (1995) people entertain themselves by reliving the recorded experiences of others. By attaching electrodes to their head, everything they see and feel is recorded for later playback. Even without the brain interface this would necessitate, we are moving closer to the point where all of our experiences are recorded, accumulated as a personal history. Already, our personal histories, as recorded on our home computers, are searchable by Google, and can be made available to the global collection of data. Those collections are growing much richer, drawing on new ways of recording our lives, and organizing that complexity is staggeringly difficult (Gemmell, Bell, & Lueder 2006).

Kevin Lim is one of many who are gradually becoming cyborgs, recording large portions of their lives. He wears a camera most days, recording his interactions with friends and strangers, while a GPS device tracks his progress through the world. Another camera sits on his desk, sending a live feed to the internet and recording his life from another angle. In this, Mr. Lim is different only in degree from the millions of people who keep public diaries of their everyday lives, and post photos and videos of their experiences. Already, this content makes up a sizable part of the web, and as "life logs" and other technologies for recording our existence grow, the data representing our everyday lives will grow with it.

Those recordings recall the Borges story in which a king orders a map at 1:1 scale to cover his entire country.[1] A recording of our life is of very little value if we can only play it back at its original speed. The idea of a perfect memory is probably more attractive than the reality might be. Russian psychologist Aleksandr Luria (2006) describes the life of a man cursed by a perfect memory, and its crippling effects. Without the ability to easily edit memories of his life experiences, he loses the ability to distinguish events and interact with the world. The solution requires that we capture the moments that we wish to remember, and delete those moments that are best forgotten without too much intervention on our part. Unfortunately, sometimes it takes us a while to know which are which. Search engine technology will be called upon to help us find valuable information in this large data stream, filtering out the normal experience of our lives to extract the most salient features.

It is hard to say whether we want to have a recording of the first glance at our future spouse, or the last conversation we have with a friend before her death. Some things may be best left to our own memories, or just beyond them. But if we are to record our lives, we will want to have search engines that manage our memories in the ways that we want, and share them only when we want them to. We are still far from having the majority of our lives recorded, but automatic metadata and analysis of video and audio recordings remain particularly important.

Beyond the search box

Current general-purpose search engines tend to "keep it simple," and attempt to connect the terms a user enters – often with very little forethought – to something that is useful. Much of the work yet to be done in search relates to extracting usable meaning and deciding how documents on the web are related, but there are also a great number of ways that information can be presented and acted upon. As search engines seek to improve searching based on user profiles and contexts, the way in which that material is displayed also depends on personal preference and the type of device that is being used. The plain vanilla search box and list of results is good enough for most devices, but are there other solutions?

For many, the ideal interface is a human, and since we already treat communication technologies as if they are humans (Reeves & Nass 1996), it makes sense to design interfaces that reflect this. Microsoft has experimented with a visual representation of a character that represents the search engine on their site, Ms. Dewey. An actress has recorded about 600 short clips that correspond to items typed into the search box and give the illusion of interactivity (Cole 2006). While it is both entertaining and intriguing to think of what a more integrated version would look like, in practice it is still just a search box. An interface that was more conversational, or one that actually used voice interaction, would run closer to this ideal – even without the visual agent. Especially for mobile devices, continued development of voice search will be vital.

Several search engines already cluster responses visually. KartOO and Mooter are among the most popular. While a number of search engines do some kind of clustering (for example, the appropriately named Clusty), the process of clustering lends itself well to graphical visualization. Touchgraph, a network graphing system, also provides an outstanding front-end for interpreting search results. These point toward future interactive graphic displays. For many, the design of the information search system depicted in the 2002 film *Minority Report* represents an ideal for interactive search. Recent work on multi-touch displays (Han 2006) and new interface metaphors has brought this ideal closer to reality. The interface that is closest to that ideal at present is the Photosynth system created by Blaise Agüera y Arcas (2007) at Microsoft Live. The system is able to gather images and sort them by space and time, so that multiple views of the same scene can be blended and arranged seamlessly. The effect is an interface that makes people think differently about what search and discovery might mean in the future.

On the other side is the need for interfaces that work on mobile and wearable systems. As the hardware for these systems changes, the need for different interfaces will emerge, but because of the size and the need for divided attention, the design of these interfaces is likely to be more iterative and linear than those that are possible in desktop environments. Such designs must make use of much less powerful displays, and limited input (Karlson et al. 2006).

Open, sociable search

There is a long history of the future of the "semantic web" (Berners-Lee, Hendler, & Lassila 2001), a future that always seems to be just over the horizon. In the meantime, we have been adding our own semantic metadata the old-fashioned way, through thick textual description and through tagging. It would be nice if we had the technology to analyze the images and sound in a YouTube video, and be able to use these data in an index. Likewise, it would be great if the creator described its contents using some form of constrained vocabulary. In practice, though, the tags that the creator and watchers provide already give a good enough indication of the meaning of the video for it to be found relatively easily by likeminded individuals. There can be little doubt that more structural approaches will evolve in a piecemeal fashion, coming first to applications where they can be particularly effective (Wayner 2007), but, on the sociable web, sociable approaches to finding meaning predominate.

The previous chapter suggests ways in which we are already moving toward sociable search. At present, social approaches to tagging and categorizing text remain the most important source of metadata on the web. By harnessing this metadata more effectively, we will be able to make inferences that actually work in the real world. Over the next few years, the most important changes in the way search is accomplished will be related to the integration of social network data with information about link networks and the content of the web. Search engines will be exploring ways in which social networking sites like Facebook and LinkedIn can be used to discover connections between resources on the web. Particularly, as ways of translating data from one social networking system to another are perfected, the social web will become even more central to search.

We will probably see continued improvements in personalization in each of the largest search engines. Personalization is a form of social search, since it relies on collaborative filtering to help to determine how a given individual will approach a novel search task. However, it is not a *sociable* search process, since the user is isolated from the other users helping to filter the search results. There is merit in this more restrictive form of collaborative filtering, but many users continue to strive for activities that will enhance their sociable use of the web.

Open-source projects are attempting to create search engines that are entirely transparent, and often calling on individuals to contribute by allowing a crawler to run from their home computer. Because the source code itself is available, the algorithms that determine how relevance is calculated are also open to observation and discussion. One of the ideas behind the engine is that open, collaborative processes can handle spam at least as well as hidden processes. There can be little doubt that opening up the ranking algorithm will make it easier to be "played"; but whether that will ultimately favor spammers remains an open question. The ideal of millions of diverse search engines running at once, each sharing its data with peers, is an enticing one (Lessig 2001, p. 137; Jeanneney, 2007).

The biggest question remains which technology will unseat Google, the behemoth. The question is asked so often that the most obvious answer is ignored: no one. The most likely path over the next decade will have Google continuing to dominate the general-purpose search market. Developments in the industry are rapid, but incremental. Each of the major players will continue to try to improve basic search, but the potential for expansion is really not at the broadest level, but in projects that can effectively exploit particular vertical search markets.

Within those markets, there will probably be significant challenges to the supremacy of the largest search engines. Many of these challengers are likely to be assimilated by one of the largest search companies, but for those who identify a specific market and dominate in that market, there is the potential to become a significant force. Baidu has already demonstrated the largest search engines' Achilles' heel: the need to appeal to everyone. By serving a particular market – even, as in Baidu's case, a particularly large market – and providing a service that is responsive to that market, it may still be possible to sneak up on the major search engines.

Who will know?

Lyotard predicted nearly thirty years ago that global computerization would give rise to new legal challenges, and, with them, the central question "Who will know?" (1984, p. 6). More recently, it has been suggested that modern military conflict will become knowledge-centric: "about who knows (or can be kept from knowing) what, when, where, and why" (Ronfeldt et al. 1998, p. 7). Search engines operate at the nexus of such questions, and those interested in shaping the future are interested in shaping search engines. If for no other reason, search engines are interesting to the person who wants to understand the exercise of power in the information society. In an era in which knowledge is the only real bankable commodity, search engines own the exchange floor. The term "search engine" is far too prosaic for the role that search plays.

In 1912, Rudyard Kipling wrote a short story called "As Easy as A.B.C." (a sequel to an earlier story entitled "With the Night Mail"), in which he gives an account of the world in the year 2000. The airplane has been overtaken by the dirigible and an "Aerial Board of Control" is established to provide global control of air traffic and "all that implies." The reliance on global transportation – especially for communication, which is handled through the mails – has led to the decline and eventual disappearance of local control, and the A.B.C. has become a global regime:

> Transportation is Civilisation, our motto runs. Theoretically we do what we please, so long as we do not interfere with the traffic and all it implies. Practically, the A.B.C. confirms or annuls all international arrangements, and, to judge from its last report, finds our tolerant, humorous, lazy little Planet

only too ready to shift the whole burden of public administration on its shoulders. (Kipling 1925)

Recent incidents provide an indication that national governments are not yet ready to cede power to the search engine giants. Nonetheless, if we wish to understand the contours of social power in the information age, we need do little more than Google it.

Notes

1 THE ENGINES

1 For a more thorough overview of the technical elements of search engine construction, see Chakrabarti (2003).

2 SEARCHING

1 www.unblinking.com/heh/googlewhack.htm.
2 See, for example, Second Life search http://secondlifesearch.blogspot.com/.
3 Google offers the oft-misspelled "Britney Spears" as an example: www.google.com/jobs/britney.html.

3 ATTENTION

1 See Adamic (n.d.) for a discussion of the relationship between Pareto distributions and the Zipf law.
2 The posting may be found at http://alex.halavais.net/how-to-cheat-good/.
3 External links only, using "link:x AND NOT site:x" searches; see Thelwall and Vaughan (2004) for discussion. Alltheweb produced similar results.
4 See, for example, Google Webmaster Guidelines, www.google.com/support/webmasters/bin/answer.py?answer=35769.

4 KNOWLEDGE AND DEMOCRACY

1 Ironically, in order to re-find this quote I turned not to the original French version of the essay, nor to my own English copy in book form, but to Google Book Search.

2 In fact, the term "ideology" is perhaps not so clearly defined. Eagleton (1991) offers no less than 21 different potential definitions, but here I intend mostly the last of these: "the process whereby social life is converted to a natural reality" (p. 2).

5 CENSORSHIP

1 Most famously the Vatican's Index Librorum Prohibitorum and Index Expurgatorius, though the term "index" was in use in other contexts as an indication of censored documents.
2 See the OpenNet Initiative (http://opennet.net/) for information on filters in various countries.
3 www.google.com/explanation.html.
4 www.chillingeffects.org/.

6 PRIVACY

1 An earlier paper published in the *Annals of Improbable Research* (Schulman, 1999) used Alta Vista to quantify fame and determine how many hits were needed to reach the "A-list."
2 See www.aolstalker.com/.
3 When first asked to provide private data to the US government in 1945, ITT Communications flatly refused. After obtaining permission to tap Western Union's lines, a representative of US intelligence went back to ITT and suggested that "his company would not desire to be the only non-cooperative company on the project" (Bamford 1983, p. 304). The situation perhaps makes clear the pressure on Google for resisting the subpoena relating to the Child Online Protection Act when Yahoo, Microsoft, and others had already complied.
4 Andrejevic (2005) provides examples of deceptive searches and secret investigations of people by other people and argues that "lateral surveillance" is merely an internalization of existing structures of control. It is important to note that the kind of transparency advocated here is open and obvious; not hidden cameras, but clearly visible cameras. When that condition is placed on lateral observation (I don't know that "surveillance" fits any longer), his argument loses some of its strength.
5 A more modest solution is proposed by Conti (2006): a browser plug-in that would catalog all the information a user was passing

to Google. He argues that, along with notification laws, this would provide more awareness of what we are giving Google and other search engines.

8 FUTURE FINDING

1 See Borges (1975). Of course, it is even more reminiscent of his short story "Funes, the Memorious" (Borges 1962), which no doubt was inspired by Luria's narrative (see below), and also ends badly for the protagonist.

Glossary

Algorithm An algorithm is any methodical way of doing things, and, in the case of search engines, usually refers to the process by which a given engine processes the data from their crawlers and determines the relevance of pages to a particular query.

Anchor text The text that is highlighted as part of a hyperlink on a page.

Archie A search engine for FTP sites.

Backlink A term used to describe a hyperlink leading to a page, rather than leading away from it.

Behavioral targeting This term refers to the ability to target particular advertising messages according to "behaviors" of a user, including visiting or viewing some combination of pages, searching for particular keywords, and the like.

Berrypicking The process of assembling the answer to a query from a diverse set of documents. Coined by Marcia Bates in 1989.

Boolean operators Words that indicate how keywords should be used by a search engine – including AND, OR, and NOT – that allow for more control over what is returned.

Clickthroughs A measurement of how many people click on an advertisement to visit the advertised site.

Cloaking Providing different version of pages to visitors who are identified as crawlers rather than as humans. This can be used by spamdexers to hide the true content of a page, but may have legitimate uses for those who wish to provide an alternative version of the page for search engines that have trouble with various formats (Flash, video, and the like).

Crawler A program that automatically follows links from page to page on the World Wide Web, recording the content of each page.

Crowdsourcing A neologism rooted in the idea of "outsourcing" large-scale production to a widely distributed group of (usually) volunteers willing to contribute a small amount of effort toward the project.

Deep link A hyperlink to a page on a website that is not the intended entry page. Search engines encourage deep linking, and some site designers and owners discourage it.

Deep web Sometimes used as an alternative to "Invisible Web," in order to clearly indicate that the pages may be visible, but that they are not indexed by the major search engines.

File Transfer Protocol (FTP) A protocol that allows for files to be uploaded and downloaded on the internet.

Golden triangle A triangular area in the upper left-hand side of (for example) a search engine results page that attracts the glance of a person's eye most readily.

Google bowling Making a competitor look like a search spammer by employing obvious spam techniques on their behalf.

Google dance The reordering of PageRank that occurred when Google completed a new crawl. Search engines now crawl continuously, so such changes are more gradual.

Googlebomb An attempt to associate a key phrase with a given website by collectively using that phrase in links to a site. The original example is linking the keyword "miserable failure" to the White House biography of George W. Bush.

Googlejuice An imaginary representation of the reputational currency provided by linking from one site to another. Such links lead to higher PageRank on Google.

Googlewack A search of two terms on Google that returns a single page as the only result. Coined by Gary Stock in 2002.

Gopher A distributed menu-driven protocol for publishing content to the internet, predating the World Wide Web.

Hits The number of results returned for a particular query. (Not to be confused with Hypertext Induced Topic Selection, or HITS, which is an algorithm developed by Jon Kleinberg designed to rank the authority of documents in a network.)

Horizontal search Search of the broader web, undertaken by general-purpose search engines, which are considered "horizontal" in order to differentiate them from search engines focused on "vertical search."

HyperText Markup Language (HTML) A set of textual "tags" that allows authors to indicate the structure of a document in such a way that it may be interpreted and displayed by a web browser.

Information foraging A theory developed by Pirolli and Card that suggests that humans search for information the way that animals search for food, making repeated, rapid decisions about the cost and potential benefit of following particular links.

Inline link The HTML code indicating the positioning of an image on a webpage includes the address where the image may be found. This is normally on the same server as the page itself, but such links can pull the image from anywhere on the web. This sort of lifting of images into a new context is sometimes called "hotlinking."

Invisible web That proportion of the web that for various reasons is not crawled and indexed by general-purpose search engines.

IP (Internet Protocol) address A unique four-digit hexadecimal code indicating a single numerical address for every device connected to the internet.

Keyword Word or series of words that make up a search engine query.

Keyword stuffing Various techniques for hiding many unrelated keywords, and often a large number of the same keyword, on a page so that it is more likely to come up as a false result when people search for those keywords.

Link farming The creation of large numbers of webpages with the single intent of linking to a particular page and making it appear popular to search engines that rely on inbound links to determine page relevance.

Link slutting (also "link whoring") Creating specific content for a site or engaging in other activities with the primary aim of collecting inbound links from other sites, and increasing Googlejuice.

Link spamming Generally, the use of links to deceive search engines as to the reputation or authority of a target website. This may also include the use of hidden links that are visible to search engines, but not to human users.

Locative media Content that is sensitive to the geographical location of the user, and responds accordingly.

Metasearch engine A search engine that accepts a query, requests results from several different search engines, and then provides the combined results.

Metatag HTML allows for tags that convey information about the page, but are not displayed on the page. These can provide a summary, relevant keywords, information about authorship, and a number of other things.

Natural Language Processing (NLP) Any attempt to extract grammatical or semantic data from "natural" human language (as opposed to computer languages).

Ontology An "ontology," within the field of computer science, refers to an explicit definition of concepts and their relationships within a particular domain. They are essential to the development of a "semantic web."

Organic search results Links from a search engine that are created as part of the natural process of search, and not, for example, as part of a paid placement, are often said to be "organic."

PageRank The Google algorithm for determining which results are most authoritative, based on the hyperlinked structure of pages linking to them.

Paid inclusion Payment guarantees a listing in a search engine, though usually not any particular ranking on the results pages.

Pay per click (PPC) Advertising paid for in terms of clickthroughs, rather than "impression," or single appearance of a message before a viewer: A common method of pricing advertising on search engines.

Permalink The URL of a blog posting that remains stable so that references to it will continue to be valid.

Power law distribution A distribution for which there exists a scale-free inverse relationship between an observed magnitude of an event and its frequency.

Preferential attachment The idea that new links in a network are likely to lead to the nodes that already enjoy a large number of backlinks.

Radio Frequency IDentification (RFID) A very small wireless beacon that allows objects to be identified from a distance.

Relevance The degree to which a search engine's results correspond to a searcher's goal.

Robot Exclusion Protocol A way for content authors to instruct crawlers which pages should and should not be indexed.

RSS A file format that packages new additions to a website over time in a format easily parsed by other applications. Abbreviation of "Really Simple Syndication," "RDF Site Summary," or "Rich Site Summary."

Scraper site A website set up to borrow content from elsewhere on the web automatically, and built with the single aim of driving up advertising revenue without producing original content.

Search engine marketing (SEM) Generally meant to include both SEO and other forms of marketing: ad placement, word-of-mouth advertising, branding, and the like.

Search engine optimization (SEO) The process (and industry) of creating pages that will receive more visibility on large search engines.

Search engine results page (SERP) A page listing the ranked results of a particular query to a search engine.

Semantic web The semantic web is a proposed way of extending the web to make it possible for computers to associate data with other data on the web, to act on that data, and to draw inferences from that data.

Spamdexing A term used to describe search spamming, or attempts to rise to the top of the search rankings for a set of keywords.

Spider *See* "Crawler."

Splog Spam blog, a blog set up in order to create links to a target page, in an effort to make it appear more authoritative and receive better placement on search engine results pages.

Stop words Words that are too common to be useful in a search, and are generally ignored by search engines.

Transaction Log Analysis (TLA) Records of many interactions on the internet, including search records, are kept in log files that can later be analyzed to provide information about search behaviors.

Uniform Resource Locator (URL) The unique web address of a given page or site, e.g.: http://alex.halavais.net.

Usenet An internet-based news forum system that reached its peak just before the World Wide Web became popular. It was initially archived on the web by Dejanews, which, when purchased by Google, eventually become Google Groups.

User-generated media A broad term taking in amateur production of media: especially things like blogs, podcasts, and shared photos and video.

Veronica A search engine that was used with Gopher.

Vertical search Search engines that limit themselves in terms of topic, medium, region, language, or some other set of constraints, and cover that area in great depth, are often called "vertical" in order to differentiate them from general-purpose search engines.

Web analytics Tools to measure and understand the behavior of users on a given website.

Web robot (or "Bot") *See* "Crawler."

Zipf Law Distribution of events such that there is an inverse relationship (with some fixed exponent) between the frequency of an event and its rank. Named for George Kingsley Zipf.

Bibliography

Abeles, T. P. 2002, "The Internet, knowledge and the academy," *foresight*, 4, 3, pp. 32–7.

Adamic, L. A. n.d., *Zipf, power-laws, and Pareto: a ranking tutorial*. Retrieved August 1, 2007, from www.hpl.hp.com/research/idl/papers/ranking/ranking.html.

Adamic, L. A. & Adar, E. 2005, "How to search a social network," *Social Networks*, 27, 3, pp. 187–203.

Adamic, L. A. & Glance, N. 2005, "The political blogosphere and the 2004 US election: divided they blog," in *3rd International Workshop on Link Discovery*, Chicago: ACM Press, pp. 36–43.

Adar, E., Weld, D. S., Bershad, B. N. & Gribble, S. D. 2007, "Why we search: visualizing and predicting user behavior," in *Proceedings of the 16th International Conference on World Wide Web (WWW '07)*, Banff: ACM Press.

Adler, S. 1999, "The Slashdot Effect, an analysis of three internet publications," *Linux Gazette*, 38.

Agre, P. 1998, "The internet and public discourse," *FirstMonday*, 3, 3. Retrieved August 1, 2007, from www.firstmonday.org/issues/issue3_3/agre/.

Agüera y Arcas, B. 2007, "Photosynth demo," presented at TED Conference, Monterey, California, February 22–25. Retrieved August 1, 2007, from www.ted.com/index.php/talks/view/id/129.

Allgrove, B. 2007, "The search engine's dilemma: implied license to crawl and cache?" *Journal of Intellectual Property Law Practice*, 2, 7, pp. 437–38.

Anakata 2004, *Re: unauthorized use of DreamWorks SKG properties*. Retrieved August 1, 2007, from http://static.thepiratebay.org/dreamworks_response.txt.

Anderson, C. 2004, "The long tail," *Wired*, 12, 10. Retrieved August 1, 2007, from www.wired.com/wired/archive/12.10/tail.html.

Anderson, N. 2007, "US intelligence wants ability to censor satellite images," *Ars Technica*, May 9. Retrieved August 1, 2007, from

http://arstechnica.com/news.ars/post/20070509-us-intelligence-
wants-ability-to-censor-satellite-images.html.

Andrejevic, M. 2005, "The work of watching one another: lateral surveillance, risk, and governance," *Surveillance & Society*, 2, 4, pp. 479–97.

Ang, P. H. & Nadarajan, B. 1996, "Censorship and the internet:
a Singapore perspective," *Communications of the ACM*, 39, 6,
pp. 72–8.

Answers.com 2007, *Answers.com Seeing Lower Traffic*, Answers.com,
from http://ir.answers.com//releaseDetail.cfm?ReleaseID=258141.

Argenti, P., MacLeod, S. & Capozzi, L. 2007, "The experts offer advice
on Google," *Journal of Business Strategy*, 28, 3, pp. 23–5.

Arlin, P. K. 1990, "Wisdom: the art of problem finding," in R. J.
Sternberg (ed.), *Wisdom: its nature, origins, and development*,
Cambridge: Cambridge University Press, pp. 23–43.

Arrington, M. 2006, "AOL proudly releases massive amounts of private data," *TechCrunch*, August 6. Retrieved August 1, 2007, from
www.techcrunch.com/2006/08/06/aol-proudly-releases-massive-
amounts-of-user-search-data.

Arroyo, E., Selker, T. & Wei, W. 2006, "Usability tool for analysis of web
designs using mouse tracks," in *Conference on Human Factors in
Computing Systems*, Montreal: ACM Press, pp. 484–9.

Aul, W. R. 1972, "Herman Hollerith," *Think*. IBM Archives, pp.
22–4, November. Retrieved August 1, 2007, from www-03.ibm.
com/ibm/history/exhibits/builders/builders_hollerith.html.

Aula, A., Jhaveri, N. & Käki, M. 2005, "Information search and re-
access strategies of experienced web users," in *Proceedings of the 14th
International Conference on the World Wide Web*, Chiba: ACM Press,
pp. 583–92.

Aula, A., Päivi, M. & Räihä, K.-J. 2005, "Eye-tracking reveals the
personal styles for search result evaluation," *Proceedings of Human–
Computer Interactions – INTERACT 2005*, Berlin: Springer,
pp. 954–7.

Bagdikian, B. H. 1983, *The media monopoly*, Boston: Beacon Press.

Bagrow, J. P. & ben-Avraham, D. 2005, "On the Google-fame of scientists and other populations," presented at 8th Granada Seminar on
Computational Physics. Retrieved August 1, 2007, from
http://arxiv.org/abs/physics/0504034.

Baksik, C. 2006, "Fair use or exploitation? The Google book search con-
troversy," *Libraries of the Academy*, 6, 4, pp. 399–415.

Balkin, J. M. 2004, "Digital speech and democratic culture: a theory of
freedom of expression for the information society," *New York
University Law Review*, 79, 1, pp. 1–55.

Bamford, J. 1983, *The puzzle palace: a report on America's most secret agency*, Harmondsworth, Middx.: Penguin Books, New York.

Band, J. 2006, "The Google library project: both sides of the story," *Plagiary: Cross-Disciplinary Studies in Plagiarism, Fabrication, and Falsification*, 1, 2, pp. 1–17.

Barbaro, M. & Zellner, T. 2006, "A face is exposed for AOL searcher 4417749," *New York Times*, August 9. Retrieved September 15, 2007, from http://query.nytimes.com/gst/fullpage.html?res=9E0CE3DD1 F3FF93AA3575BC0A9609C8B63.

Barber, B. R. 1996, *Jihad vs. McWorld*, New York: Ballantine Books.

Barlow, J. P. 1996, *A declaration of the independence of cyberspace*, Electronic Frontier Foundation. Retrieved August 1, 2007, from http://homes.eff.org/~barlow/Declaration-Final.html.

Bar-Zeev, A. 2007, "The value of censoring Google Earth," *RealityPrime*, July 9. Retrieved August 1, 2007, from www.realityprime.com/articles/the-value-of-censoring-google-earth.

Bates, M. J. 1989, "The design of browsing and berrypicking techniques for the online search interface," *Online Review*, 13, 5, pp. 407–24.

Battelle, J. 2005, *The search: how Google and its rivals rewrote the rules of business and transformed our culture*, New York: Portfolio.

Bauman, Z. 2000, *Liquid modernity*, Cambridge: Polity.

Becerra-Fernandez, I. 2006, "Searching for experts on the web: A review of contemporary expertise locator systems," *ACM Transactions on Internet Technology*, 6, 4, pp. 333–55.

Becker, D. 2004, "Google caught in anti-Semitism flap," *ZDNet*, April 7. Retrieved August 1, 2007, from http://news.zdnet.com/2100-3513-22-5186012.html.

Beitzel, S. M., Jensen, E. C., Chowdhury, A., Grossman, D. & Ophir, F. 2004, "Hourly analysis of a very large topically categorized web query log," in *Proceedings of the 27th Annual International ACM SIGIR Conference on Research and Development in Information Retrieval*, Sheffield: ACM Press.

Belkin, N. J., Oddy, R. N. & Brooks, H. M. 1982, "ASK for information retrieval: Part I: Background and theory," *Journal of Documentation*, 38, 2, pp. 61–71.

Bender, W. 2002, "Twenty years of personalization: all about the 'Daily Me,'" *Educause Review*, 37, 5, pp. 21–9.

Benkler, Y. 2006, *The wealth of networks: how social production transforms markets and freedom*, New Haven: Yale University Press.

Benway, J. P. & Lane, D. M. 1998, "Banner blindness: we searchers often miss 'obvious' links," *Internetworking*, 1, 3. Retrieved August

1, 2007, from www.internettg.org/newsletter/dec98/banner_blind-ness.html.

Benyon, D. 1998, "Cognitive engineering as the development of information spaces," *Ergonomics*, 41, 2, pp. 153–5.

Berners-Lee, T., Hendler, J. & Lassila, O. 2001, "The semantic web," *Scientific American*, 284, 5, pp. 34–43.

Bharat, K. & Broder, A. 1998, "A technique for measuring the relative size and overlap of public Web search engines," *Computer Networks and ISDN Systems*, 30, 1–7, pp. 379–88.

Bishop, T. 2007, "Google takes its ad system into the video-game market," *Seattle P-I*, July 18. Retrieved August 1, 2007, from http://seattlepi.nwsource.com/business/324213_googleads19.html.

Biundo, J. & Enge, E. 2006, *Creating advanced custom search engines*. Retrieved August 1, 2007, from http://blogoscoped.com/archive/2006–11–15-n50.html.

Blake, W. 1982, *The complete poetry and prose of William Blake*, Berkeley: University of California Press.

Blanke, T. 2005, "Ethical subjectification and search engines: ethics reconsidered," *International Review of Information Ethics*, 3, pp. 33–8.

Blanzieri, E. & Giorgini, P. 2000, "From collaborative filtering to implicit culture: a general agent-based framework," presented at the Workshop on Agents and Recommender Systems, Barcelona, from http://asteseer.ist.psu.edu/271576.html.

Bogatin, D. & Sullivan, D. 2007, "Open debate," in *Fast Company*, p. 116. Retrieved August 1, 2007, from www.fastcompany.com/magazine/113/open_open-debate.html?partner=rss.

Boguslaw, R. 1971, "Systems of power and the power of systems," in A. Westin (ed.), *Information technology in a democracy*, Cambridge, Mass.: Harvard University Press, pp. 419–31.

Borges, J. L. 1962, "Funes, the memorious," in *Ficciones*, New York: Grove Press, pp. 107–16.

1975, "Of exactitude in science," in *A Universal History of Infamy*, Harmondsworth, Middx.: Penguin, p. 131.

Bourdieu, P. 1986, "The forms of capital," in J. Richardson (ed.), *Handbook of theory and research for the sociology of education*, New York: Greenwood Press, pp. 241–58.

2000, *Pascalian meditations*, Stanford: Stanford University Press.

2003, "The Berber house," in S. M. Low & D. Lawrence-Zúñiga (eds.), *The anthropology of space and place: locating culture*, Malden, Mass.: Blackwell, pp. 131–41.

Bowman, C. M., Danzig, P. B., Manber, U. & Schwartz, M. F. 1994, "Scalable internet resource discovery: research problems and approaches," *Communications of the ACM*, 37, 8, pp. 98–107, 114.

Boydell, O. & Smyth, B. 2007, "From social bookmarking to social summarization: an experiment in community-based summary generation," in *Proceedings of the 12th International Conference on Intelligent User Interfaces*. Honolulu: ACM Press, pp. 42–51.

Brand, S. 1987, *The Media Lab: inventing the future at MIT*, New York: Viking.

Brenner, D. L. 1996, *Law and regulation of common carriers in the communications industry*, Boulder: Westview Press.

Brewer, E. 2001, "When everything is searchable," *Communications of the ACM*, 44, 3, pp. 53–5.

Brin, D. 1998, *The transparent society: will technology force us to choose between privacy and freedom?* Reading, Mass.: Perseus Books.

Brin, S. & Page, L. 1998, "The anatomy of a large-scale hypertextual web search engine," *Computer Networks*, 30, 1–7, pp. 107–17.

Broder, A. 2002, "A taxonomy of web search," *ACM SIGIR Forum*, 36, 2, pp. 3–10.

Broder, A., Kumar, R., Maghoul, F., Raghavan, P., Rajagopalan, S., Stata, R., Tomkins, A. & Wiener, J. 2000, "Graph structure in the Web," *Computer Networks*, 33, 1–6, pp. 309–20.

Brooks, F. P. 1995, *The mythical man-month: essays on software engineering*, anniversary edn., Reading, Mass.: Addison-Wesley Pub. Co.

Brophy, J. & Bawden, D. 2005, "Is Google enough? Comparison of an internet search engine with academic library resources," *Aslib Proceedings: New Information Perspectives*, 57, 6, pp. 498–512.

Brown, D. J. 2004, "Web search considered harmful," *Queue*, 2, 2, pp. 84–3.

Brynjolfsson, E., Hu, Y. J. & Smith, M. D. 2003, "Consumer surplus in the digital economy: estimating the value of increased product variety at online booksellers," *MIT Sloan Working Paper*, vol. 4305-03. Retrieved August 1, 2007, from http://papers.ssrn.com/sol3/papers.cfm?abstract_id=400940.

Buckley, C. & Rashbaum, W. K. 2007, "4 men accused of plot to blow up Kennedy airport terminals and fuel lines," *New York Times*, June 3. Retrieved August 1, 2007, from www.nytimes.com/2007/06/03/nyregion/03plot.html.

Burton, J. 1972, *World society*, Cambridge: Cambridge University Press.

Bush, V. 1945, "As we may think," *Atlantic Monthly*, 176, July, pp. 101–8.

Calishain, T. 2007, *Information trapping: real-time research on the web*, Berkeley, Calif.: New Riders.

Calore, M. 2007, "Yahoo's new suggested search feature is half-baked," *Wired News "Compiler,"* July 12. http://blog.wired.com/monkey-bites/2007/07/yahoos-new-sugg.html.

Campbell-Kelly, M. & Aspray, W. 1996, *Computer: a history of the information machine*, New York: Basic Books.

Capra, R. G. & Pérez-Quiñones, M. A. 2005, "Using web search engines to find and refind information," *IEEE Computer*, 38, 10, pp. 36–42.

Carey, J. 1969, "The communications revolution and the professional communicator," *Sociological Review Monograph*, 13, pp. 23–8.

Carmel, Y. & Ben-Haim, Y. 2005, "Info-gap robust-satisficing model of foraging behavior: do foragers optimize or satisfice?" *American Naturalist*, 166, 5, pp. 634–41.

Caufield, J. 2005, "Where did Google get its value?" *Libraries and the Academy*, 5, 4, pp. 555–72.

Chakrabarti, S. 2003, *Mining the Web: discovering knowledge from hypertext data*, San Francisco, Calif.: Morgan Kaufmann Publishers.

Chellapilla, K. & Chickering, D. M. 2006, "Improving cloaking detection using search query popularity and monetizability," presented at 2nd International Workshop on Adversarial Information Retrieval on the Web, Seattle, August 10, 2006.

Cheng, J. 2007, "1-800-GOOG-411 brings Google search to voice calls," *Ars Technica*, April 9. Retrieved August 1, 2007, from http://arstechnica.com/news.ars/post/20070409-google-rolls-out-free-411-service.html.

Chi, E. H. & Pirolli, P. 2006, "Social information foraging and collaborative search," presented at HCIC Workshop, Fraser, Colorado, USA.

Cho, C.-H. & Cheon, H. J. 2004, "Why do people avoid advertising on the internet?" *Journal of Advertising*, 33, 4, pp. 89–97.

Cho, J. & Roy, S. 2004, "Impact of search engines on page popularity," in *Proceedings of the 13th International Conference on World Wide Web*, New York: ACM Press, pp. 20–9.

Church, K., Smyth, B., Cotter, P. & Bradley, K. 2007, "Mobile information access: a study of emerging search behavior on the mobile internet," *ACM Transactions on the Web*, 1, 1, pp. 1–38.

Clarke, R. 1988, "Information technology and dataveillance," *Communications of the ACM*, 31, 5, pp. 498–512.

Cohen, B. 1963, *The press and foreign policy*, Princeton: Princeton University Press.

Cole, S. 2006, "Spending time with Ms. Dewey," *Marketplace*, December 13. Retrieved August 1, 2007, from http://marketplace.publicradio.org/shows/2006/12/13/PM200612138.html.

Colin, C. 2007, "Pig balls and stuck skunks: a 311 customer service rep has a window onto San Francisco's secret heart," *SFGate*. Retrieved September 5, 2007, from www.sfgate.com/cgi-bin/article.cgi?f=/g/a/2007/09/04/onthejob.DTL.

comScore, July 1, 2007, "Key measurements," 2007. Retrieved August 1, 2007, from www.comscore.com/press/data.asp.

comScore, July 9, 2007, "comScore publishes the first comprehensive review of Asia-Pacific internet usage," *Press Release*, 2007. Retrieved August 1, 2007, from www.comscore.com/press/release.asp?press=1520.

Conti, G. 2006, "Googling considered harmful," in *Proceedings of the 2006 Workshop on New Security Paradigms*, New York: ACM Press, pp. 67–76.

Cooper, J. F. 2004, *The American democrat* (1938), New York: Barnes & Noble Books.

Cutts, M., Moulton, R. & Carattini, K. 2007, "A quick word about Googlebombs," *Webmaster Central Blog*, January 25. Retrieved August 1, 2007, from http://googlewebmastercentral.blogspot.com/2007/01/quick-word-about-googlebombs.html.

Czitrom, D. J. 1982, *Media and the American mind: from Morse to McLuhan*, Chapel Hill: University of North Carolina Press.

Daniel, C. & Palmer, M. 2007, "Google's goal: to organize your daily life," *Financial Times*. Retrieved August 1, 2007, from www.ft.com/cms/s/2/c3e49548–088e-11dc-b11e-000b5df10621.html.

Davenport, T. H. & Beck, J. C. 2001, *The attention economy: understanding the new currency of business*, Cambridge, Mass.: Harvard Business School Press.

Davison, B. D., Najork, M. & Converse, T. 2006, "Adversarial information retrieval on the web," *ACM SIGIR Forum*, 40, 2, pp. 27–30.

Department of Trade and Industry 2006, *Consultation document on the electronic commerce directive: the liability of hyperlinkers, location tool services and content aggregators, Government response and summary of responses*, December. Retrieved December 15, 2007, from www.berr.gov.uk/files/file35905.pdf.

Deutsch, K. 1966, *The nerves of government: models of political communication and control*, New York: The Free Press.

Deutsch, P. 2000, "Archie: a Darwinian development process," *Internet Computing*, 4, 1, pp. 89–97.

Deutschman, A. 2007, "Why is this man smiling?" *Fast Company*, 114, p. 62. Retrieved August 1, 2007, from www.fastcompany.com/magazine/114/features-why-is-this-man-smiling.html.

Dewey, J. 1927, *The public and its problems*, New York: H. Holt & Co.

Dickinson, A., Smith, M., Arnott, N. & Robin, H. 2007, "Approaches to web search and navigation for older computer novices," in *SIGCHI Conference on Human Factors in Computing Systems*, San Jose, Calif.: ACM Press, pp. 281–90.

DiMaggio, P., Hargittai, E., Celeset, C. & Shafer, S. 2004, "Digital inequality: from unequal access to differentiated use," in K. Neckerman (ed.), *Social inequality*, New York: Russell Sage Foundation, pp. 355–400.

DiMaggio, P., Hargittai, E., Neuman, W. R. & Robinson, J. P. 2001, "Social implications of the internet," *Annual Review of Sociology*, 27, pp. 307–36.

Dittenbach, M., Berger, H. & Merkl, D. 2006, "Automated concept discovery from web resources," in *Proceedings of the 2006 IEEE/WIC/ACM International Conference on Web Intelligence*, Washington, D.C.: IEEE Computer Society, pp. 309–12.

Doctorow, C. 2003, *Down and out in the Magic Kingdom*, New York: Tor.
2007, "Scroogled," *Radar*, September 12. Retrieved September 15, 2007, from www.radaronline.com/from-the-magazine/2007/09/ google_fiction_evil_dangerous_surveillance_control_1.php.

Donath, J. 2004, "Sociable media," in W. S. Bainbridge (ed.), *The encyclopedia of human–computer interaction*, Great Barrington, Mass.: Berkshire Publishing Group.

Eagleton, T. 1991, *Ideology: an introduction*, London: Verso.

Eco, U. 1989, *Foucalt's pendulum*, New York: Harcourt.
1995, *The search for the perfect language*, Oxford: Blackwell.

Edwards, J. 2007, "Google, DoubleClick throw punches in privacy war," *Adweek.com*, July 16.

Eichmann, D. 1994, "The RBSE spider: balancing effective search against web load," *Computer Networks and ISDN Systems*, 4, 2, pp. 281–8.

Eisenstein, E. L. 1979, *The printing press as an agent of change: communications and cultural transformations in early modern Europe*, Cambridge: Cambridge University Press.

Elmer, G. 2006, "The vertical (layered) net)," in D. Silver & A. Massanari (ed.), *Critical cyberculture studies*, New York: New York University Press.

Engelbart, D. & Lehtman, H. 1988, "Working together," *BYTE*, 13, 13, pp. 245–52.

Erickson, T. 1996, "The World-Wide Web as social hypertext," *Communications of the ACM*, 39, 1, pp. 15–17.

Erickson, T. & Kellogg, W. 2000, "Social translucence: an approach to designing systems that support social processes," *ACM Transactions on Computer–Human Interaction*, 7, 1, pp. 59–83.

Etzioni, A. 1999, *The limits of privacy*, New York: Basic Books.

Ewen, S. 1976, *Captains of consciousness*, New York: McGraw-Hill.

Fallows, D. 2005, *Search engine users*, Pew Internet and American Life, Washington, D.C. Retrieved August 1, 2007, from www.pewinternet.org/pdfs/PIP_Searchengine_users.pdf.

Farrell, W. 1998, *How hits happen*, New York: HarperBusiness.

Finkelstein, S. 2003, *Chester's guide to molesting Google*. Retrieved August 1, 2007, from http://sethf.com/anticensorware/general/chester.php.

Fishkin, R. & Pollard, J. 2007, *Search engine ranking factors v2*, SEOmoz. Retrieved December 15, from www.seomoz.org/article/search-ranking-factors.

Foley, M. W. & Edwards, B. 1999, "Is it time to disinvest in social capital?" *Journal of Public Policy*, 19, pp. 141–73.

Freeman, E. & Freeman, E. 2006, *Head first HTML with CSS & XHTML*, Sebastopol, Calif. and Beijing: O'Reilly.

Freyne, J., Farzan, R., Brusilovsky, P., Smyth, B. & Coyle, M. 2007, "Collecting community wisdom: integrating social search and social navigation," in *12th International Conference on Intelligent User Interfaces*, Honolulu: ACM Press, pp. 52–61.

Fry, J. 2006, "Google's privacy responsibilities at home and abroad," *Journal of Librarianship and Information Science*, 38, 3, pp. 135–9.

Fulgoni, G. 2007, *Younger consumers receptive to advertising on user-generated content sites*. Retrieved December 15, from www.comscore.com/blog/2007/05/younger_consumers_receptive_to.html.

Galin, J. R. & Latchaw, J. 1998, "Heterotopic spaces online: a new paradigm for academic scholarship and publication," *Kairos*, 3, 1. Retrieved December 15, from http://english.ttu.edu/kairos/3.1/binder2.html?coverweb/galin/index.htm.

Gardner, H. 1983, *Frames of mind: the theory of multiple intelligences*, New York: Basic Books.

Geertz, C. 1983, *Local knowledge*, New York: Basic Books.

Gemmell, J., Bell, G. & Lueder, R. 2006, "MyLifeBits: a personal database for everything," *Communications of the ACM*, 49, 1, pp. 88–95.

Gershenfeld, N. A. 2005, *Fab: the coming revolution on your desktop – from personal computers to personal fabrication*, New York: Basic Books.

Gibson, O. 2006, "Google to appeal, as court rules news site is illegal," *Guardian International*, September 19. Retrieved August 1, 2007, from www.guardian.co.uk/international/story/0,,1875616,00.html.

Giddens, A. 1984, *The constitution of society*, Berkeley, Calif.: University of California Press.

Ginsparg, P. 1996, "Winners and losers in the global research village," *UNESCO scientists' view of electronic publishing and issues raised*,

UNESCO, Paris. Retrieved August 1, 2007, from http:// people.ccmr.cornell.edu/~ginsparg/blurb/pg96unesco.html.

Glaser, M. 2005, "Companies subvert search results to squelch criticism," *Online Journalism Review*, June 1. Retrieved December 15, from www.ojr.org/ojr/stories/050601glaser/.

Goffman, E. 1997, "Self-presentation," in E. Goffman, C. C. Lemert & A. Branaman (eds.), *The Goffman Reader*, Oxford: Blackwell, pp. 21–6.

Goldhaber, M. H. 1997, "The attention economy and the net," *FirstMonday*, 2, 4, p. 1. Retrieved August 1, 2007, from www.firstmonday.org/issues/issue2_4/goldhaber/.

Goldman, E. 2005, "Search engine bias and the demise of search engine utopianism," *Yale Journal of Law & Technology*, 8, pp. 188–200.

Google 2007, *Corporate Information*, July 1. Retrieved August 1, 2007 from www.google.com/corporate/history.html.

"Google y Yahoo, denunciados ante Consumo por publicidad engañosa," 2007, *El Pais.com*, August 13, 2007. Retrieved December 15, 2007 from www.elpais.com/articulo/internet/Google/Yahoo/denunciados/Consumo/publicidad/enganosa/elpeputec/20070813 elpepunet_6/Tes.

Gordon, M., Lindsay, R. K. & Fan, W. 2002, "Literature-based discovery on the World Wide Web," *ACM Transactions on Internet Technology*, 2, 4, pp. 261–75.

Gori, M. & Numerico, T. 2003, "Social networks and web minorities," *Cognitive Systems Research*, 4, 4, pp. 355–64.

Gori, M. & Witten, I. 2005, "The bubble of web visibility: promoting visibility as seen through the unique lens of search engines," *Communications of the ACM*, 48, 3, pp. 115–17.

Gorman, G. E. 2006, "Giving way to Google," *Online Information Review*, 30, 2, pp. 97–9.

Graham, L. & Metaxas, P. T. 2003, " 'Of course it's true; I saw it on the Internet!': critical thinking in the internet era," *Communications of the ACM*, 46, 5, pp. 70–5.

Gramsci, A. 1957, *The modern prince and other writings*, New York: International Publishers.

Granka, L. A., Joachims, T. & Gay, G. 2004, "Eye-tracking analysis of user behavior in WWW search," in *Proceedings of the 27th Annual International ACM SIGIR Conference on Research and Development in Information Retrieval*, New York: ACM Press, pp. 478–9.

Greenberg, A. 2007, "Condemned to Google hell," *Forbes.com*, April 30. Retrieved August 1, 2007, from www.forbes.com/2007/04/29/sanar-google-skyfacet-tech-cx_ag_0430googhell.html?partner=rss.

Grimmelmann, J. T. 2008, "The structure of search engine law," *Iowa Law Review*, 93. Retrieved September 15, 2007, from http://ssrn.com/abstract=979568.

Guan, Z. & Cutrell, E. 2007, "An eye tracking study of the effect of target rank on web search," in *Proceedings of the SIGCHI Conference on Human Factors in Computing Systems*, San Jose, Calif.: ACM Press, pp. 417–20.

Guinee, K., Eagleton, M. B. & Hall, T. E. 2003, "Adolescents' internet search strategies: drawing upon familiar cognitive paradigms when accessing electronic information sources," *Journal of Educational Computing Research*, 29, 3, pp. 363–74.

Hachten, W. A. 1992, *The world news prism*, 5th edn., Ames: Iowa State University Press.

Haigh, G. 2006, "Information idol: how Google is making us stupid," *Monthly*, 9, pp. 25–33. Retrieved August 1, 2007, from www.themonthly.com.au/tm/?q=node/170.

Haines, L. 2005, "US rolls out robotic broadband airship," *Register*, April 13. Retrieved August 1, 2007, from www.theregister.co.uk/2005/04/13/broadband_airship/.

Halavais, A. 2000, "National borders on the World Wide Web," *New Media and Society*, 2, 1, pp. 7–28.
    2006, "The visible college: blogs as transparent research journals," in A. Bruns & J. Jacobs (eds.), *Uses of blogs*, New York: Peter Lang, pp. 117–26.
    2008, "The hyperlink as organizing principle," in J. Turow & L. Tsui (eds.), *The hyperlinked society: questioning connections in the digital age*, Ann Arbor: University of Michigan Press.

Han, J. 2006, *Multi-touch interaction research*. Retrieved August 1, 2007, from http://cs.nyu.edu/~jhan/ftirtouch/.

Hansell, S. 2007, "Google keeps tweaking its search engine," *New York Times*, June 3. www.nytimes.com/2007/06/03/business/your-money/03google.html.

Hargittai, E. 2002a, "Second-level digital divide: differences in people's online skills," *FirstMonday*, 7, 4. http://firstmonday.org/issues/issue7_4/hargittai/.
    2002b, "Beyond logs and surveys: in-depth measures of people's online skills," *Journal of the American Society of Information Science and Technology*, 53, 14, pp. 1239–44.

Hargittai, E. 2004, "Do you 'Google?' Understanding search engine use beyond the hype," *FirstMonday*, 9, 3. Retrieved December 15, 2007, from www.firstmonday.org/issues/issue9_3/hargittai/index.html.

Hargittai, E. 2006, "Hurdles to information seeking: spelling and typographical mistakes during users' online behavior," *Journal of the Association of Information Systems*, 7, 1, pp. 52–67.

2008, "The role of experience in navigating links of influence," in J. Turow & L. Tsui (eds.), *The hyperlinked society: questioning connections in the digital age*, Ann Arbor: University of Michigan Press.

Harper, J. 2007, "Google 'get a life': ignore the roar of the JFK plotters," *National Review Online*. Retrieved August 1, 2007, from http://article.nationalreview.com/?q=Zjg4YmZhYjJmYzQyNTU5NzllZjY2ZjI4Y2I3NzQwZDc=.

Harris, S. 2006, "TIA lives on," *National Journal*. Retrieved August 1, 2007, from http://nationaljournal.com/about/njweekly/stories/2006/0223nj1.htm.

Hartnick, A. J. 2007, "Intellectual property," *New York Law Journal*, October 18.

Hearing of the Africa, Global Human Rights and International Operations Subcommittee of the House International Relations Committee: The Internet in China, a tool for freedom or suppression, February 15, 2006. Retrieved from the Federal News Service, November, 1, 2006.

Heine, C. 2007, *Five things today's digital generation cannot do*, 21st Century Information Fluency Project / Illinois Mathematics and Science Academy. Retrieved August 1, 2007, from http://21cif.imsa.edu/resources/features/leadarticle_v1_no.html.

Herper, M. 2007, "Google's genetic start-up," *Forbes.com*, September 12. Retrieved September 12, 2007, from www.forbes.com/business/2007/09/12/genomics-wojcicki-brin-biz-sci-cx_mh_0912_23andme.html.

Heyamoto, L. 2007, "How to best your Google twin," *Chicago Sun-Times*, March 14. Retrieved August 1, 2007, from http://findarticles.com/p/articles/mi_qn4155/is_20070314/ai_n18715436.

Hindman, M., Tsioutsiouliklis, K. & Johnson, J. A. 2003, *"Googlearchy": how a few heavily-linked sites dominate politics on the web*. Retrieved August 1, 2007, from www.cs.princeton.edu/~kt/mpsa03.pdf.

Hines, J. 2007, Remarks in panel session: Beyond Simple Search, at Director of National Intelligence Conference on Open Source Intelligence, Washington, D. C., July 16–17.

Hinman, L. M. 2005, "Esse est indicato in Google: ethical and political issues in search engines," *International Review of Information Ethics*, 3, pp. 19–25.

Hitwise, 2007, *Google receives 64 percent of all U.S. searches in August 2007*. Retrieved September 20, 2007, from www.hitwise.com/press-center/hitwiseHS2004/ussearchenginesaugust20070920.php.

Hogan, C. 1998, *Search engine survey: prospect researchers report their favorites*, PRSPCT-L. Retrieved August 1, 2007, from www2.ups.edu/our/adi/research/survey.htm.

Holderness, M. 1998, "Who are the world's information-poor?" in B. D. Loader (ed.), *Cyberspace divide*, London: Routledge.

Hölscher, C. & Strube, G. 2000, "Web search behavior of Internet experts and newbies," *Computer Networks*, 33, 1, pp. 337–46.

Howard, P. & Massanari, A. 2007, "Learning to search and searching to learn: income, education, and experience online," *Journal of Computer-Mediated Communication*, 12, 3, p. 5. Retrieved August 1, 2007, from http://jcmc.indiana.edu/vol12/issue3/howard.html.

Howe, A. E. & Dreilinger, D. 1997, "SavvySearch: a metasearch engine that learns which search engines to query," *AI Magazine*, 18, pp. 19–25.

Howe, J. 2006, "The rise of crowdsourcing," *Wired*, 14, 6. Retrieved August 1, 2007, from www.wired.com/wired/archive/14.06/crowds.html.

Hoyt, C. 2007, "When bad news follows you," *New York Times*, August 26. Retrieved August 26, 2007, from www.nytimes.com/2007/08/26/opinion/26pubed.html?_r=1&oref=slogin.

Huberman, B. A. 2001, *The laws of the Web: patterns in the ecology of information*, Cambridge, Mass.: MIT Press.

Huberman, B. A., Pirolli, P. L. T., Pitkow, J. E. & Lukose, R. M. 1998, "Strong regularities in World Wide Web surfing," *Science*, 280, pp. 95–7.

Hugo, V. 1999, *Notre-Dame de Paris*, Oxford: Oxford University Press.

Introna, L. D. & Nissenbaum, H. 2000, "Shaping the web: why the politics of search engines matters," *The Information Society*, 16, 3, pp. 169–85.

James, B. 1995, "The Web: out of the lab and spun around the world," *International Herald Tribune*, March 20. Retrieved August 1, 2007, from www.iht.com/articles/1995/03/20/web.php.

Jansen, B. J. 2003, "Operators not needed? The impact of query structure on web searching results," in *Information Resource Management Association International Conference*, Hainburg, Penn.: Idea Group, pp. 814–17.

Jansen, B. J. & Pooch, U. 2000, "Web user studies: a review and framework for future work," *Journal of the American Society of Information Science and Technology*, 52, 3, pp. 235–46.

Jansen, B. J., Spink, A. & Saracevic, T. 2000, "Real life, real users, and real needs: a study and analysis of user queries on the web," *Information Processing & Management*, 36, pp. 207–27.

Jasco, P. 2005, "As we may search: comparison of major features of the Web of Science, Scopus, and Google Scholar citation-based and citation-enhanced databases," *Current Science*, 89, 9, pp. 1537–47.

Jeanneney, J. N. 2007, *Google and the myth of universal knowledge*, trans. T. L. Fagan, Chicago: University of Chicago Press.

Jefferson, T. 1903, *The writings of Thomas Jefferson*, Washington, D.C.

Joachims, T., Granka, L. A., Pan, B., Hembrooke, H., Radlinski, F. & Gay, G. 2007, "Evaluating the accuracy of implicit feedback from clicks and query reformulations in web search," *ACM Transactions on Information Systems*, 25, 2, pp. 7, 1–27.

Johnson, D. G. 1997, "Is the Global Information Infrastructure a democratic technology?" *Computers and Society*, 27, 3, pp. 20–6.

Jones, M., Buchanan, G., Harper, R. & Xech, P.-L. 2007, "Questions not answers: a novel mobile search technique," in *Proceedings of the SIGCHI Conference on Human Factors in Computing Systems*, New York: ACM Press, pp. 155–8.

Jupiter Communications 1999, "Europeans opt for local eMerchants," *NUA Internet Surveys*, October 4. Retrieved August 1, 2007, from web.archive.org/web/20000308035434/www.nua.ie/surveys/?f=VS &art_id=905355317&rel=true.

Kane, L. T. 1997, "Access vs. ownership: do we have to make a choice," *College & Research Libraries*, 58, 1, pp. 59–67.

Karlson, A. K., Robertson, G. G., Robbins, D. C., Czerwinski, M. P. & Smith, G. R. 2006, "FaThumb: a facet-based interface for mobile search," in *SIGCHI Conference in Human Factors in Computing Systems*, Montreal, Quebec, Canada: ACM Press, pp. 711–20.

Kaser, D. 1962, "In principium erat verbum," *Peabody Journal of Education*, 39, 5, pp. 258–63.

Kautz, H., Selman, B. & Shah, M. 1997, "Referral Web: combining social networks and collaborative filtering," *Communications of the ACM*, 40, 3, pp. 63–5.

Kellner, D. 1997, "Intellectuals, the new public spheres, and techno-politics," in C. Toulouse & T. W. Luke (eds.), *The politics of cyberspace: a new political science reader*, London: Routledge, pp. 167–86.

Kenney, B. 2004, "Googlizers vs. resistors", *Library Journal*, December 15. Retrieved August 1, 2007, from www.libraryjournal.com/article/CA485756.html.

Kinzie, S. & Nakashima, E. 2007, "Calling in prose to refine your Google image," *Washington Post*, July 2, p. A01. Retrieved August 1, 2007, from www.washingtonpost.com/wp-dyn/content/article/2007/07/01/AR2007070101355.html.

Kipling, R. 1925, "As easy as A.B.C." in *A diversity of creatures: letters of travel, 1892–1913*, Garden City, N.Y.: Doubleday.

Klein, G. A. 1999, *Sources of power: how people make decisions*, Cambridge, Mass.: MIT Press.

Kleinberg, J. M. 1999, "Authoritative sources in a hyperlinked environment," *Journal of the ACM*, 46, 5, pp. 604–32.

Kornhauser, W. 1960, *The politics of mass society*, London: Routledge.

Krug, S. 2006, *Don't make me think!: a common sense approach to Web usability*, 2nd edn., Berkeley, Calif.: New Riders Pub.

Kumar, R., Ragbaven, P., Rajagopalan, S. & Tomkins, A. 2002, "The Web and social networks," *IEEE Computer*, 35, 11, pp. 32–6.

Labbo, L. D., Reinking, D. & McKenna, M. C. 1998, "Literacy education in the 21st century," *Peabody Journal of Education*, 73, 3/4, pp. 273–89.

Lampe, C., Ellison, N. & Steinfield, C. 2006, "A face(book) in the crowd: social searching vs. social browsing," *20th Anniversary Conference on Computer Supported Cooperative Work*, Banff, Alberta, Canada: ACM Press, pp. 167–70.

Law, J. 1989, "Technology and heterogeneous engineering: the case of Portuguese expansion," in W. Bijker, T. Hughes & T. Pinch (eds.), *The social construction of technological systems: new directions in the sociology and history of technology*, Cambridge, Mass.: MIT Press.

Leary, P. 2005, "Googling the Victorians," *Journal of Victorian Culture*, 10, 1, pp. 72–86.

Lenhart, A., Horrigan, J. & Fallows, D. 2004, *Content creation online*, Pew Internet & American Life Washington, D.C. Retrieved August 1, 2007, from www.pewinternet.org/report_display.asp?r=113.

Lenhart, A., Simon, M. & Graziano, M. 2001, *The internet and education*, Pew Internet and American Life, Washington, D.C. Retrieved August 1, 2007, from www.pewinternet.org/report_display.asp?r=39.

Lessig, L. 2001, *The future of ideas*, New York: Vintage.

Levin, D. & Arafeh, S. 2002, *The digital disconnect: the widening gap between internet-savvy students and their schools*, Pew Internet and American Life, Washington, D.C. Retrieved August 1, 2007, from www.pewinternet.org/report_display.asp?r=67.

Lévy, P. 1997, *Collective intelligence: mankind's emerging world in cyberspace*, Cambridge, Mass.: Perseus Books.

Lewis, C. & Fabos, B. 2005, "Instant messaging, literacies, and social identities," *Reading Research Quarterly*, 40, 4, pp. 470–501.

Liebel, U., Kindler, B. & Pepperkok, R. 2005, "Bioinformatic 'Harvester': a search engine for genome-wide human, mouse, and rat protein resources," *Methods in Enzymology*, 404, pp. 19–26.

Lithwick, D. 2003, "Google-Opoly: the game no one but Google can play," *Slate*, January 29. Retrieved August 1, 2007, from www.slate.com/id/2077875/.

Ljunggren, D. 2007, "Global web privacy rules needed in 5 years: Google," *Reuters*, September 24. Retrieved September 24, 2007, from www.reuters.com/article/internetNews/idUSN24299593 20070924?sp=true.

Long, J., Skoudis, E. & van Eikelenborg, A. 2005, *Google hacking for penetration testers*, Rockland, Md.: Syngress.

Long, P. D. 2002, "OpenCourseWare: simple idea, profound implications," *Syllabus*, 15, 6, pp. 12–14.

Luria, A. R. 2006, *The mind of a mnemonist: a little book about a vast memory*, Cambridge, Mass.: Harvard University Press.

Lyotard, J.-F. 1984, *The postmodern condition*, Minneapolis: University of Minnesota Press.

Machill, M. & Beiler, M. 2006, "Internet-Suchmaschinen als neue Herausforderung für die Medienregulierung: Jugendschutz und publizistische Vielfalt als Fallbeispiele für Governance Issues," *Von der Medienpolitik zur Media Governance? Neue Problemstellungen, Ansätze und Formen der Regulierung öffentlicher Kommunikation*, Zurich. Retrieved August 1, 2007, from www.mediapolicy.unizh.ch/tagungen/mediagovernance/abstract_machill_beiler.pdf.

Machill, M., Neuberger, C. & Schindler, F. 2002, *Transparenz im Netz: Funktionen und Defizite von Internet-Suchmaschinen*, Gütersloh: Verlag Bertelsmann Stiftung.

Madden, M. 2005, *Do-it-yourself information online*, Pew Internet & American Life, Washington, D.C. Retrieved August 1, 2007, from www.pewinternet.org/report_display.asp?r=157.

Mahle, M. B. 2006, *Denial and deception: an insider's view of the CIA*, New York: Nation Books.

Mann, S., Nolan, J. & Wellman, B. 2003, "Sousveillance: inventing and using wearable computing devices for data collection in surveillance environments," *Surveillance & Society*, 1, 3, pp. 331–55.

Marcuse, H. 1964, *One-dimensional man*, Boston: Beacon Press.

Marvin, C. 1988, *When old technologies were new: thinking about electric communication in the late nineteenth century*, New York: Oxford University Press.

Mattelart, A. 2000, *Networking the world: 1794–2000*, trans. L. Carey-Libbrecht & J. A. Cohen, Minneapolis: University of Minnesota Press.

Mayclim, T. 2006, *Growing number of job searches disrupted by digital dirt*, Execunet. Retrieved August 1, 2007, from www.execunet.com/m_releases_content.cfm?id=3349.

McChesney, R. R. 1996, "The Internet and U.S. communication policy-making in historical and critical perspective," *Journal of Communication*, 46, 1, pp. 98–124.

McCullagh, D. 2006, "AOL's disturbing glimpse into users' lives," *CNET News.com*, August 7. Retrieved August 1, 2007, from http://news.cnet.com/2100-1030_3-6103098.html.

McCullagh, D. & Mills, E. 2006, "Feds take porn fight to Google," *CNET News.com*, January 19. Retrieved August 1, 2007, from www.news.com/Feds-take-porn-fight-to-Google/2100-1030_3-6028701.html.

McFedries, P. 2003, "Google this," *IEEE Spectrum*, 40, 2, p. 68.

McHugh, J. 2003, "Google vs. evil," *Wired*, 11, 1, from www.wired.com/wired/archive/11.01/google_pr.html.

McLuhan, M. 1962, *The Gutenberg galaxy: the making of typographic man*, Toronto: University of Toronto Press.

McPherson, M., Smith-Lovin, L. & Cook, J. M. 2001, "Birds of a feather: homophily in social networks," *Annual Review of Sociology*, 27, pp. 415–44.

Merton, R. K. & Barber, E. 2003, *The travels and adventures of serendipity: a study in sociological semantics and the sociology of science*, Princeton: Princeton University Press.

Meyer, J. 2006, "France searches for its own Google," *Business Week*, March 30. Retrieved August 1, 2007, from www.businessweek.com/globalbiz/content/mar2006/gb20060330_385311.htm.

Miles, S. 2006, "Google delists BMW Germany for foul play," in *Pocket-lint*, February 5. Retrieved August 1, 2007, from www.pocket-lint.co.uk/news/news.phtml/2404/3428/bmw-germany-google-ranking-search.phtml.

Milewski, R. J. 2006, "Automatic recognition of handwritten medical forms for search engines," Ph. D. dissertation, State University of New York at Buffalo, AAT 3226605.

Miller, G. A. 1956, "The magical number seven, plus or minus two: some limits on our capacity for processing information," *Psychological Review*, 63, pp. 84–97.

Mills, C. W. 1959, *The sociological imagination*, New York: Oxford University Press.

Mislove, A., Gummadi, K. & Druschel, P. 2006, "Exploiting social networks for internet search," presented at the Fifth Workshop on Hot Topics in Networks, Irvine, California, November 29–30.

Mowshowitz, A. & Kawaguchi, A. 2002, "Bias on the web," *Communications of the ACM*, 45, 9, pp. 56–60.

Mumford, L. 1964, "Authoritarian and democratic technics," *Technology and culture*, 5, 1, pp. 1–8.

Munro, A., Höök, K. & Benyon, D. 1999, *Social navigation of information space*, London: Springer.

Nathanson, I. S. 1998, "Internet infoglut and invisible ink: spamdexing search engines with meta tags," *Harvard Journal of Law & Technology*, 12, 1.

Nielsen, J. 2003, "Diversity is power for specialized sites," *Alertbox*, June 16. Retrieved August 1, 2007, from www.useit.com/alertbox/20030616.html.

2005, "Mental models for search are getting firmer," *Alertbox*, May 9. Retrieved August 1, 2007, from www.useit.com/alertbox/20050509.html.

Noam, E. 1997, "An unfettered internet? Keep dreaming," *New York Times*, July 11. Retrieved September 20, 2007, from http://query.nytimes.com/gst/fullpage.html?res=9D01E7DF1139F932A25754C0A961958260.

Noruzi, A. 2004, "Application of Ranganathan's laws of the web," *Webology*, 2, 1. Retrieved August 1, 2007, from www.webology.ir/2004/vin2/a8.html.

Ntoulas, A., Zerfos, P. & Cho, J. 2005, "Downloading textual hidden web content through keyword queries," in *Proceedings of the Joint Conference on Digital Libraries (JCDL)*, New York: ACM Press, pp. 100–9.

Orlowski, A. 2003, "Google to fix blog noise problem," *Register*, May 9. Retrieved August 1, 2007, from www.theregister.co.uk/2003/05/09/google_to_fix_blog_noise/.

Page, L., Brin, S., Motwani, R. & Winograd, T. 1998, *The PageRank citation ranking: bringing order to the web*, Stanford Digital Library Technologies Project. Retrieved August 1, 2007, from http://dbpubs.stanford.edu:8090/pub/1999-66.

Pandey, S., Roy, S., Olston, C., Cho, J. & Chakrabarti, S. 2005, "Shuffling a stacked deck: the case for partially randomized ranking of search engine results," in *31st International Conference on Very Large Data Bases*, Norway: Trondheim, pp. 781–92.

Pandurangan, G., Raghavan, P. & Upfal, E. 2002, "Using PageRank to characterize web structure," in *Computing and Combinatorics: 8th*

Annual International Conference, COCOON 2002, Singapore, August 15–17, 2002. Proceedings, Springer, Heidelberg, pp. 1–4.

Parekh, B. 2000, Rethinking multiculturalism: cultural diversity and political theory, Cambridge, Mass.: Harvard University Press.

Parker, G. 1994, Internet Guide: Veronica, Education Library, Vanderbilt University. Retrieved August 1, 2007, from www.lib.umich.edu/govdocs/godort/archive/elec/intveron.txt.old.

Pasquale, F. A. & Bracha, O. 2007, "Federal search commission? Access, fairness and accountability in the law of search," University of Texas Law, Public Law Research Paper No. 123. Available at SSRN: http://ssrn.com/abstract=1002453.

Pedone, M. 2005, Google bowling: how competitors can sabotage you, Webpronews.com. Retrieved August 1, 2007, from www.webpronews.com/expertarticles/2005/10/27/google-bowling-how-competitors-can-sabotage-you-what-google-should-do-about-it.

Pennock, D. M., Flake, G. W., Lawrence, S., Glover, E. J. & Giles, C. L. 2002, "Winners don't take all: characterizing the competition for links on the web," Proceedings of the National Academy of Sciences of the United States of America, 99, 8, pp. 5207–11.

Penzias, A. 1989, Ideas and information, New York: Simon & Schuster.

Peters, J. D. 1999, Speaking into the air: a history of the idea of communication, Chicago: University of Chicago Press.

Peters, T. 1997, "The brand called you," Fast Company, 10, p. 83. Retrieved August 1, 2007, from www.fastcompany.com/online/10/brandyou.html.

Pinkerton, B. 1994, "Finding what people want: experiences with the WebCrawler," presented at the Second World Wide Web Conference, Chicago, October 17–19.

Pirolli, P. & Card, S. K. 1999, "Information foraging," Psychological Review, 106, pp. 643–75.

Pitkow, J. E., Schütze, H., Cass, T., Cooley, R., Turnbull, D., Edmonds, A., Adar, E. & Breuel, T. 2002, "Personalized search: a contextual computing approach may prove a breakthrough in personalized search efficiency," Communications of the ACM, 45, 9, pp. 50–5.

Plato 2002, Phaedrus, New York: Oxford University Press.

Plotz, R. 1997, "Positive spin: Senate campaigning on the Web," PS: Political Science and Politics, 30, 3, pp. 482–6.

Polanyi, M. 1998, Personal knowledge (1952), London: Routledge.

Pool, I. de S. 1983, Technologies of freedom, Cambridge, Mass.: Belknap Press.

Poor, N. 2005, "Mechanisms of an online public sphere: the Slashdot website," Journal of Computer-Mediated Communication, 10, 2, p. 4.

Poster, M. 2006, *Information please: culture and politics in the age of digital machines*, Durham, N. C.: Duke University Press.

Prensky, M. 2001, "Digital natives, digital immigrants," *On the Horizon*, 9, 5, pp. 1–2. Retrieved August 1, 2007, from www.marcprensky.com/writing/Prensky%20-%20Digital%20Natives,%20Digital%20Immigrants%20-%20Part1.pdf.

— 2004, "The emerging online life of the digital native." Retrieved August 1, 2007, from www.marcprensky.com/writing/Prensky-The_Emerging_Online_Life_of_the_Digital_Native-03.pdf.

Putnam, R. 1995, "Bowling alone: America's declining social capital," *Journal of Democracy*, 6, 1, pp. 65–78.

Qui, J. L. 2000, "Virtual censorship in China: keeping the gate between cyberspaces," *International Journal of Communications Law and Policy*, 4. Retrieved August 1, 2007, from www.ijclp.org/4_2000/ijclp_webdoc_1_4_2000.html.

Rainie, L. 2005, *Search engine use shoots up in the past year and edges towards email as the primary internet application*, Pew Internet & American Life, Washington, D. C. Retrieved August 1, 2007, from www.pewinternet.org/report_display.asp?r=167.

— 2007, *28% of online Americans have used the internet to tag content*, Pew Internet & American Life, Washington, D. C. Retrieved August 1, 2007, from www.pewinternet.org/report_display.asp?r=201.

Ramirez, A., Walther, J. B., Burgoon, J. K. & Sunnafrank, M. 2002, "Information-seeking strategies, uncertainty, and computer-mediated-communication: toward a conceptual model," *Human Communication Research*, 28, 2, pp. 213–28.

Ratzan, L. 2006, "Mining the deep web: search strategies that work," *Computerworld*, December 11. www.computerworld.com/action/article.do?command=viewArticleBasic&articleId=9005757.

Rees-Mogg, W. 2006, "Grow up, Google: you've accepted censorship, now confront copyright," *The Times*, January 30, Features, p. 21.

Reeves, B. & Nass, C. 1996, *The media equation: how people treat computers, television, and new media like real people and places*, Cambridge: Cambridge University Press.

Regan, K. 2005, "Vertical search market quickly becoming crowded," *E-Commerce Times*, April 3. Retrieved August 1, 2007, from www.ecommercetimes.com/story/41982.html/.

Ribak, A., Jacovi, M. & Soroka, V. 2002, "'Ask before you search': peer support and community building with ReachOut," in *ACM Conference on Computer Supported Cooperative Work*, New Orleans: ACM Press, pp. 126–35.

Robins, K. & Webster F. 1999, *Times of the technoculture: from the information society to the virtual life*, London: Routledge.

Ronfeldt, D. F., Arquilla, J., Fuller, G. E. & Fuller, M. 1998, *The Zapatista "Social Netwar" in Mexico*, Santa Monica, Calif.: RAND.

Rowlands, I. & Nicholas, D. 2005, "Scholarly communication in the digital environment," *Aslib Proceedings: New Information Perspectives*, 57, 6, pp. 481–97.

Rowley, J. 2002, "'Window' shopping and browsing opportunities in cyberspace," *Journal of Consumer Behavior*, 1, 4, pp. 369–78.

Rust, R. T. & Oliver, R. W. 1994, "The death of advertising," *Journal of Advertising*, 23, 4, pp. 71–7.

Salton, G. 1975, *A theory of indexing*, Philadelphia: Society for Industrial and Applied Mathematics.

Schenker, J. L. 2006, "What Google can't do," *Red Herring*, December 25. www.redherring.com/Article.aspx?a=20376.

Schiller, H. I. 1971, *Mass communication and American empire*, Boston: Beacon Press.

  1996, *Information inequality: the deepening social crisis in America*, London: Routledge.

Schudson, M. 1978, *Discovering the news: a social history of American newspapers*, New York: Basic Books.

  1997, "Why conversation is not the soul of democracy," *Critical Studies in Mass Communication*, 14, 4, pp. 297–309.

Schuler, D. 2001, "Computer professionals and the next culture of democracy," *Communications of the ACM*, 44, 1, pp. 52–7.

Schulman, E. 1999, "Can fame be measured quantitatively?" *Annals of Improbable Research*, 5, 3, p. 16.

Schulz, D., Burgard, W., Fox, D., Thrun, S. & Cremers, A. B. 2000, "Web interfaces for mobile robots in public places," *IEEE Robotics & Automation Magazine*, 7, 1, pp. 48–56.

Schwartz, M. F. & Leyden, P. 1997, "The long boom: a history of the future: 1980–2020," *Wired*, 5, 7, from www.wired.com/wired/archive/5.07/longboom/html.

Sennett, R. 2008, *The craftsman*, New Haven: Yale University Press.

Shah, R. 2000, *History of the Finger Protocol*. Retrieved August 1, 2007, from www.rajivshah.com/Case_Studies/Finger/Finger.htm.

Shakespeare, W. 1912, *Troilus and Cressida*, New York: The Macmillan Company.

Shenk, D. 1997, *Data smog: surviving the information glut*, San Francisco: Harper Edge.

Sherman, C. & Price, G. 2001, *The Invisible Web: uncovering information sources search engines can't see*, Medford, N.J.: CyberAge Books.

Shneiderman, B. 2000, "Universal usability," *Communications of the ACM*, 43, 5, pp. 84–91.

Silverstein, C., Marais, H., Henzinger, M. & Moricz, M. 1999, "Analysis of a very large web search engine query log," *ACM SIGIR Forum*, 33, 1, pp. 6–12.

Simmel, G. 1964, *Conflict: the web of group-affiliations*, New York: Free Press.

Simon, H. A. 1956, "Rational choice and the structure of the environment," *Psychological Review*, 63, 2, pp. 129–38.

1969, *The sciences of the artificial*, Cambridge, Mass.: MIT Press.

1971, "Designing organizations for an information-rich world," in M. Greenberger (ed.), *Computers, communications, and the public interest*, Baltimore: The Johns Hopkins University Press, pp. 37–72.

Singel, R. 2006, "AT&T seeks to hide spy docs," *Wired News*, April 12. Retrieved August 1, 2007, from www.wired.com/science/discoveries/news/2006/04/70650.

Sklair, L. 1995, *Sociology of the global system*, 2nd edn., Baltimore: The Johns Hopkins University Press.

Smith, J. F. 1964, "Systematic serendipity," *Chemical & Engineering News*, 42, 35, pp. 55–6.

Snyder, H. & Rosenbaum, H. 1997, *How public is the Web?: robots, access, and scholarly communication*, Center for Social Informatics, Bloomington, WP-98-05. Retrieved August 1, 2007, from https://scholarworks.ice.edu/dspace/html/2022/1099/wp98-05B.html.

Sokullu, E. 2007, "Competing with Google search," *Read/WriteWeb*, July 18. Retrieved August 1, 2007, from www.readwriteweb.com/archives/competing_with_google_search.php.

Solomon, L. 2007, "LSD as therapy? Write about it, get barred from US," *The Tyee*, April 23. Retrieved September 15, 2007, from http://thetyee.ca/News/2007/04/23/Feldmar/.

Spaink, K. & Hardy, C. 2002, *Freedom of the internet: our new challenge*, Organization for Security and Co-operation in Europe. Retrieved August 1, 2007, from www.spaink.net/english/osce-form pdf.

Specter, M. 2007, "Damn spam: the losing war on junk email," *New Yorker*, 83, pp. 36–40. Retrieved August 1, 2007, from www.newyorker.com/reporting/2007/08/06/070806fa_fact_specter.

Spink, A., Jansen, B. J., Wolfram, D. & Saracevic, T. 2002, "From e-sex to e-commerce: Web search changes," *IEEE Computer*, 35, 3, pp. 107–9.

Sterling, G. 2007, "Will Google remain 'The start page for the internet'?" *Search Engine Land*, February 8. Retrieved August 1, 2007, from http://searchengineland.com/070208–120621.php.

"Street advertising gets local-stock-savvy" 2007, *New Scientist*, January 10, p. 21. www.newscientisttech.com/article/mg19325854.900-street-advertising-gets-localstocksavvy.html.

Suber, P. 2007, "Trends favoring open access," *CTWatch Quarterly*, 3, 3. Retrieved September 18, 2007, from www.ctwatch.org/quarterly/articles/2007/08/trends-favoring-open-access/3/.

Sullivan, D. 2000, "Invisible web gets deeper," *Search Engine Watch*, August 2. Retrieved August 1, 2007, from http://searchenginewatch.com/showPage.html?page=2162871.

2007, "Top 10 search providers, July 2007," *Search Engine Watch*, August 30. Retrieved September 10, 2007, from http://searchenginewatch.com/showPage.html?page=3626903.

Sunstein, C. R. 2001, *Republic.com*, Princeton: Princeton University Press.

2006, *Infotopia*, New York: Oxford University Press.

Svensson, M., Höök, K., Laaksolahti, J. & Waern, A. 2001, "Social navigation of food recipes," in *SIGCHI Conference on Human Factors in Computing Systems*, Seattle: ACM Press, pp. 341–8.

Swidey, N. 2003, "A nation of voyeurs: how the internet search engine Google is changing what we can find out about another – and raising questions about whether we should," *Boston Globe*, Magazine, February 2, p. 10.

Tatum, C. 2005, "Deconstructing Google bombs: a breach of symbolic power or just a goofy prank?" *First Monday*, 10, 10. Retrieved August 1, 2007, from www.firstmonday.org/issues/issue10_10/tatum/.

Thelwall, M. n.d., "Extracting accurate and complete results from search engines: case study Windows Live," *Journal of the American Society of Information Science and Technology*. Retrieved August 1, 2007, from www.scit.wlv.ac.uk/~cm1993/mycv.html.

Thelwall, M. & Vaughan, L. 2004, "A fair history of the Web? Examining country balance in the Internet Archive," *Library & Information Science Research*, 26, 2, pp. 162–76.

Tobin, J. 1998, "An American otaku (or, a boy's virtual life on the Net)," in J. Sefton-Green (ed.), *Digital diversions: youth culture in the age of multimedia*, London: Routledge.

Tönnies, F. 1957, *Community and society (Gemeinschaft und Gesellschaft)*, East Lansing: Michigan State University Press.

Tung, L. 2007, "Australia sets date for Google keyword case," *ZD Net*, November 19. Retrieved December 15, 2007, from http://news.zdnet.co.uk/internet/0,1000000097,39290916,00.htm.

Turkle, S. 1996, "Rethinking identity through virtual community," in L. Hershman-Leeson (ed.), *Clicking in: hot links to a digital culture*, Seattle: Bay Press, pp. 116–22.

Turner, L. 2007, "Does negative press make you Sicko?" *Google Health Advertising Blog*, June 29. Retrieved August 1, 2007, from http://google-health-ads.blogspot.com/2007/06/does-negative-press-make-you-sicko.html.

Twist, J. 2005, "Looming pitfalls of work blogs," *BBC News*, January 3. Retrieved August 1, 2007, from http://news.bbc.co.uk/2/hi/technology/4115073.stm.

US Congress Committee on International Relations 2006, "The internet in China: a tool for freedom or suppression." Retrieved August 1, 2007, from www.foreignaffairs.house.gov/archives/109/26075.pdf.

Vaas, L. 2005, "Blogger blocked at US border," *eWeek.com*, November 29. Retrieved September 15, 2007, from www.eweek.com/article2/0,1759,1894227,00.asp?kc=EWRSS03119TX1K0000594.

Vadén, T. & Suoranta, J. 2004, "Breaking radical monopolies: towards political economy of digital literacy," *E-Learning*, 1, 2, pp. 283–301.

Vaidhyanathan, S. 2007, "The Googlization of everything and the future of copyright," *University of California, Davis Law Review*, 40, 3, pp. 1207–31.

Valentine, M. B. 2005, *Playing in Googlebot's sandbox with Slurp, Teoma, MSNbot: spiders display distinctly differing personalities*, Publish 101. Retrieved July 1, 2007, from http://rss.publish101.com/business/Pages-Slurp-Teoma-Site-Search-112391.html.

Van Alstyne, M. & Brynjolfsson, E. 1996, "Could the internet Balkanize science?" *Science*, 274, 5292, pp. 1479–89.

Vander Wal, T. 2005, *Folksonomy definition and Wikipedia*. Retrieved August 1, 2007, from www.vanderwal.net/random/entrysel.php?blog=1750.

Vaughan, L. & Thelwall, M. 2004, "Search engine coverage bias: evidence and possible causes," *Information Processing & Management*, 40, 4, pp. 693–707.

Vredenburg, K., Isensee, S. & Righi, C. 2001, *User-centered design: an integrated approach*, Prentice Hall PTR, New Jersey: Upper Saddle River.

Walker, C. W. 2004, "Application of the DMCA safe harbor provisions to search engines," *Virginia Journal of Law & Technology*, 9.

Walker, J. 2005, "Links and power: the political economy of linking on the web," *Library Trends*, 53, 4, pp. 524–9.

Walther, J. B. 1996, "Computer-mediated communication: impersonal, interpersonal, and hyperpersonal interaction," *Communication Research*, 23, 1, pp. 3–43.

Warf, B. & Grimes, J. 1997, "Counterhegemonic discourses and the internet," *Geographical Review*, 87, 2, pp. 259–74.

Wayner, P. 2007, "Helping computers to search with nuance, like us," *New York Times*, September 12. Retrieved September 15, 2007, from www.nytimes.com/2007/09/12/technology/techspecial/12soft.html.

Webber, S. 2002, "Mapping a path to the empowered searcher," in C. Graham (ed.), *Online Information 2002: proceedings*, London: Learned Information Europe. pp. 177–81.

Weinberger, D. 2007, *Everything is miscellaneous: the power of the new digital disorder*, New York: Times Books.

Weinstein, L. 2007, "Search engine dispute notifications: request for comments," *Lauren Weinstein's Blog*, June 15. Retrieved August 1, 2007, from http://lauren.vortex.com/archive/000253.html.

Westerman, S. J., Hambly, S., Alder, C., Wyatt-Millington, C. W., Shrayne, N. M., Crawshaw, C. M. & Hockey, G. R. J. 1996, "Investigating the human–computer interface using the Datalogger," *Behavior Research Methods, Instruments, & Computers*, 28, 4, pp. 603–6.

Whetstone, R. 2006, "About the Google News case in Belgium," *The Official Google Blog*, September 25. Retrieved December 15, 2007, from http://googleblog.blogspot.com/2006/09/about-google-news-case-in-belgium.html.

Wiggins, R. 2003, "The privilege of ranking: Google plays ball," *Searcher*, 11, 7. Retrieved August 1, 2007, from www.infotoday.com/searcher/jul03/wiggins.shtml.

Williams, M. 2005, "Wireless broadband takes to the sky in Japan," *Computerworld*. Retrieved August 1, 2007, from www.computerworld.com/mobiletopics/mobile/story/0,10801,105758,00.html.

Winner, L. 1980, "Do artifacts have politics?" *Daedalus*, 109, 1, pp. 121–36.

1995, "Who will we be in cyberspace?" *Information Society*, 12, 1, pp. 63–72.

1997, "Cyberlibertarian myths and the prospects for community," *Computers and Society*, 27, 3, pp. 14–19.

Yanbe, Y., Jatowt, A., Nakamura, S. & Tanaka, K. 2007, "Can social bookmarking enhance search in the web?" *International Conference on Digital Libraries*, Vancouver, BC, Canada: ACM Press, pp. 107–16.

Yates, J. 1982, "From press book and pigeonhole to vertical filing: revolution in storage and access systems for correspondence," *Journal of Business Communication*, 19, 3, pp. 5–26.

Yeo, G. 1995, "The soul of cyberspace," *New Perspectives Quarterly*, 12, 4.

Yuwono, B., Lan, S. L. Y., Ying, J. H. & Lee, D. L. 1995, "A World Wide Web resource discovery system," presented at The Fourth International World Wide Web Conference, Boston, December 11–14.

Retrieved August 1, 2007, from www.w3.org/Conferences/WWW4/Papers/66/.

Zeller, T. 2006, "AOL executive quits after posting of search data," *International Herald Tribune*, August 22. Retrieved August 1, 2007, from www.iht.com/articles/2006/08/22/business/aol.php.

Zhang, J. & Ackerman, M. S. 2005, "Searching for expertise in social networks: a simulation of potential strategies," in *Proceedings of ACM SIGGROUP Conference on Supporting Group Work*, New York: ACM Press, pp. 71–80.

Zhang, Y. 2001, "Scholarly use of internet-based electronic resources," *Journal of the American Society of Information Science and Technology*, 52, 8, pp. 628–54.

Zillmer, N. & Furlong, B. 2006, *The emerging opportunity in vertical search (updated)*, Chicago: SearchChannel and Slack Barshinger.

Zimmer, M. 2008, "The externalities of search 2.0: the emerging privacy threats when the drive for the perfect search engine meets web 2.0," *First Monday*, 13, 3. Retrieved March 15, 2008, from www.uic.edu/htbin/cgiwrap/bin/ojs/index.php/fm/article/view/2136/1944.

Zipf, G. K. 1949, *Human behavior and the principle of least effort: an introduction to human ecology*, Cambridge, Mass.: Addison-Wesley.

Zittrain, J. & Edelman, B. 2003, "Empirical analysis of internet filtering in China," *IEEE Internet Computing* 7, 2, pp. 70–7.

Zuboff, S. & Maxmin, J. 2002, *The support economy*, New York: Viking.

Index